WALKING THE WAY

Walking the Way

81 Zen Encounters
with the
Tao Te Ching

Robert Meikyo Rosenbaum
Foreword by Sojun Mel Weitsman

WISDOM PUBLICATIONS • BOSTON

Wisdom Publications
199 Elm Street
Somerville, MA 02144 USA
www.wisdompubs.org

Library of Congress
Cataloging-in-Publication Data
Rosenbaum, Robert.
 Walking the way : 81 Zen encounters with
the Tao Te Ching / Robert Meikyo Rosen-
baum ; foreword by Sojun Mel Weitsman.
    pages cm
 Includes bibliographical references and
index.
 ISBN 1-61429-025-3 (pbk. : alk. paper)
 1. Zen Buddhism—Relations—Taoism.
 2. Taoism—Relations—Zen Buddhism. 3.
Laozi. Dao de jing. I. Title.
 BQ9269.4.T3R68 2013
 294.3'444—dc23

2012037700

ISBN 978-1-61429-025-4
eBook ISBN 978-1-61429-026-1

17 16 15 14 13
5 4 3 2 1

Cover design by Phil Pascuzzo.
Caligraphies by Shodo Harada, courtesy of
One Drop Zendo Association.
Interior design by Gopa&Ted2.
Set in Janson Text LT Std 10.4/15.5.

This book is for my daughters.

Table of Contents

Foreword

> The being of a thing makes it handy;
> its nonbeing lets it function.
>
> —Tao Te Ching

WHAT I HAVE always found so impressive about the Tao Te Ching is its profound simplicity. It's like coming across an ancient, weathered, solitary pine that exists above the tree line that whistles the tunes of the wind on a high mountain; it endures throughout space and time. Formed by the elements, it speaks of the harmonious interplay between heaven and earth.

Around the fourth and fifth centuries c.e., Buddhism was beginning to gain a foothold among the intellectuals and aristocracy in China. Yet the Indian scholars had a difficult time communicating the ideas written in the Sanskrit Buddhist scriptures to the Chinese. Because Chinese Taoist concepts were closest to Indian Buddhist concepts, especially the Prajna Paramita texts, the Indian scholars chose to use Taoist terms to express the Dharma. This system was called *ke-yi*, which means "matching terms," or "analogy."

Later, in the sixth century c.e., Buddhism in China separated from the Tao of Laotze and Chuangtze, and came to be understood more on its own terms. Nevertheless, the mutual influence of Taoism and Buddhism on each other continued to be a major factor in the emergence of the form of Buddhism that came to be known as Zen. It is a characteristic of Buddhism to assimilate appropriate cultural icons in a country where the Dharma arrives and to give them a place in their "pantheon." As an example, the use of the term Tao, signifying the Way, is shared by both Buddhists and Taoists.

A major text of the Chinese Tsaodong school of Zen (Jap. Soto) is the *Can Tong Qui* (Jap. Sandokai), translated as *The Merging of Difference and Unity*, written by Shitou Xiquian (Jap. Sekito Kisen). Although it is a Buddhist text, the title was taken from a Taoist book. My late teacher Shunryu Suzuki, when asked if it was a Buddhist or a Taoist text, said that when a Taoist reads it, it is a Taoist text, and when a Buddhist reads it, it is a Buddhist text. Eternal truths are all-encompassing and so are able to be expressed through the lens of a relative place and time.

Immersed as we are in our busy schedules, crammed into date-books and calendars, we sometimes lose track of how our lives play out against the background of eternity. Let me share with you one way I think about these qualities of time, specifically with regard to clocks and watches.

I am old enough to remember when digital clocks first made their appearance, tuning us in on "horizontal" time by isolating just one number for our convenience. For many of us it was a shock. I felt that something important was lost in just that single summary number—but I wasn't sure why. Now I realize that although horizontal time is convenient for knowing when to do what, in a certain way it also isolates us from the whole picture.

What does a round clock, an analog clock, tell us about time? The clock face is an empty circle with a hub at its center. This circle gives form to time but because it is not yet divided it is an indicator of unified time, eternal time. We put numbers all around the circumference, and moving hands to illustrate the hours and minutes. Even so, right at the center of the clock is a still point, the fundamental truth of the moment. When we have the awareness of momentary time against the background of unified time, a clock becomes a wonderful example of the harmony of the temporal and the eternal.

No matter what time it is, it is always just now. Each moment is a moment of eternal time. This is stillness at the center of activity and activity as a function of stillness. The Tao Te Ching is like this.

The author of the present book, Robert Rosenbaum, is a long-time Zen Buddhist practitioner, qigong teacher, and psychotherapist. He has been inspired by the teachings and wisdom of Laotze and Chuangtze to contemplate his life and life's work through the eyes of those ancient sages. In doing so, he presents eighty-one Taoist poems along with his own insights and understanding of them in a running commentary drawn from everyday life: family, work, and Dharma experiences.

The eighty-one poems from the Tao Te Ching are, to me, like a solitary mountain against a clear sky, and Bob's comments and stories are like the earth and moving water at its foot. Through this work, we see how Taoism and Buddhism complement each other, how both have shaped the author's life, and how they can do so for us as well.

Both the Tao and the Dharma tell us that the most obvious truth is right in front of our face and to look for it here—not over there. As we all know, it is the space between the notes that makes the music.

This book is a labor of love and respect, an offering to the great Taoist sages of the past, and to you, the reader. Please enjoy.

Sojun Mel Weitsman is a former abbot
of the San Francisco Zen Center

Introduction

ZEN ASKS EACH OF US: how do you realize your original self? The eighty-one chapters of the Tao Te Ching offer us a guide to doing this naturally, with effortless effort. Because being yourself is ultimately Being itself, the Tao Te Ching is not a "how to" manual; it is an invitation for us to practice finding our Way.

In this book I do not provide scholarly explanations of the Tao Te Ching's verses: many resources provide that better than I can, and a full understanding of all the verses would be the work of many lifetimes. Instead, inspired by a line or a phrase, I offer you fragments of Zen, bits of psychology, some word play, an occasional neuropsychological finding, some poetry, and even a few jokes. Hopefully all this will induce some curiosity and perhaps even some creative confusion that will encourage you to playfully practice being yourself.

I hope you enjoy the journey as much as I have.

ABOUT THE TAO TE CHING AND ITS AUTHOR

Lao Tzu, the name traditionally given to the author of the Tao Te Ching, simply means "Old Master"—yet there are indications the author of the Tao Te Ching was an actual person. According to legend somewhere around 516 B.C.E. an eighty-eight-year-old archivist, witnessing the decline of the state of Chou, left his post there and journeyed toward his home town of Husien. When he reached the cloud-tossed pass of Hanku, the pass-keeper recognized him as a sage and said to him: "You are about to retire. Please force yourself to write a book for me." Lao Tzu sat down, wrote a book expounding Tao and Te and then—as an excellent example to all would-be future teachers—departed, never to be seen again. In the felicitous phrase of the translator Red Pine, Lao Tzu "achieved anonymity as well as immortality."

Over the next thousand years, these eighty-one verses (which eventually came to be called the Tao Te Ching) became part of the shared experience of the Chinese people. The words and their underlying spirit suffused the soul of Chinese society; they appear in the highest cultured literature as well as in the humblest folk sayings.

Together with the texts of Chuang Tzu and Lieh Tzu, the Lao Tzu text formed the basis of the first phase of Taoism. Taoism as a religion later evolved into multivarious, often esoteric forms; it became a complement as well as a contrast to the other two main strands of Chinese spirituality (Confucianism and Buddhism). The fundamental simplicity of the Tao Te Ching, however—its deep respect for what is most basic and "just natural" in the flow of existence, and the manner in which this can be expressed harmoniously—always remained as an undercurrent beneath the vagaries of passing fashion.

The Chan masters of Tang Dynasty China had the Tao in their bloodstream. Though the exact nature of the relationship between Buddhism and Taoism might be a subject of considerable dispute from both sides, the deeper our familiarity with Tao and Te, the closer we can come to the experience of our Zen ancestors and the wisdom of Zen: the ungraspable reality of our original self.

A NOTE ON THE TRANSLATION

The Tao Te Ching is a much-translated and therefore widely varying work; both the content and structure changes substantially across translations. In working with Lao Tzu's text I found I needed to read multiple translations, take some time to digest them and then, meditating on each verse without thinking about it too much (or too little), write a bit about how it spoke to me. I compiled my own version of each verse by consulting a number of translations (the ten main translations I used appear in the bibliography).

The version I have created is emphatically not a scholarly one. It tries to stay faithful to the original but I sometimes use poetic license to convey the meaning that seems most important to me. Occasionally I take a bit of liberty and use a Zen allusion in a line or two, or give the interpretation a bit more Zen flavor than the original might hold. Forty years' experience as a Zen student has, I'm afraid, tinted me a bit. Zen has deep roots in the Tao, but I hope to have written this in such a way that you do not need to be familiar with the special language of either Zen or Tao to understand the content.

Most versions of the Tao Te Ching divide it into parts: one on Tao ("the Way"), one on *Te* (usually translated as "Virtue," but I prefer to use the term "Rightness"). Experts disagree on what the original order of the verses may have been. Some texts place Te before Tao, but I have followed the more common custom of putting Tao first.

In fact, the divisions are not so straightforward. If one groups the verses solely on the basis of content, the traditional ordering breaks down. It might be clearer for the purposes of exposition to cluster the material by common themes, but Lao Tzu's verses create their own mysterious path in the order in which they usually appear, a path which is barely discernible by explicit logic yet one which is still felt on some deeper, less discursive level. So in Parts I and II you will find Te is in Tao and Tao is within Te, and that is how it should be.

SUGGESTIONS FOR READING THIS BOOK

Each chapter consists of a verse from the Tao Te Ching followed by an essay on some aspects of the verse as it relates to being yourself, concluding with a personal anecdote. There is no need to read through the verses in sequence (though I've found that if you do so, a subtle thread links them harmoniously). Feel free to wander as you read, sampling chapters and verses as they speak to you.

It is probably best to take a verse at a time; let yourself absorb it intuitively, without thinking too hard about it. When something opens up, it can be good to linger; when something puzzles, it can be helpful to move on. Returning to what was obscure at a later time, you may be surprised to find new clarity in both the verse and yourself.

ACKNOWLEDGMENTS

I'm grateful to my sweetheart, Jeanne Courtney, for her unflagging support through my ups and downs. I also owe her a particular debt: sitting by her bookshelf one day, I noticed she had several copies of Chuang Tzu and I started to thumb through them idly. They spoke strongly to me, and this began my return to the Tao.

I am grateful for the acceptance and gentle guidance of my Zen teacher Sojun Mel Weitsman and my Dayan Qigong teacher Master Hui Liu. They have tolerated and encouraged me through many years of practice.

My daughters have kept me honest and brought me renewal and delight; my sister and brother-in-law have been unswerving in their loving support and encouragement. My colleagues in psychology, neurology, and medicine have inspired me with their selfless devotion to the well-being of all the people they minister to, and my fellow practitioners at Berkeley and San Francisco Zen Centers and at the Wen Wu School have supported me with the examples of their strong ongoing practice.

I recently read of the death of Henry Littlefield, a teacher in my high school and assistant dean where I went to college. He taught me *yoga* means *union*, and showed me a path of gentle compassion leavened by a wicked sense of humor. He also taught me that if you sign up for something wondering whether the cost will be worth it, it probably won't be.

I want to extend special thanks to friends who have read and offered feedback on early versions of this manuscript: David Levitin, Belinda Khong, Art Bohart, Susan Moon, Colleen Busch, Janet Roth.

Calligraphy by Shodo Harada

Part I: Tao ～ The Way

The character for Tao can be literally translated as "path." In the context of Lao Tzu, it usually is translated as "Way," with connotations of Nature or the Absolute—a field far beyond form and emptiness in which the life and death of all beings takes place. Tao is both the river in which we are swimming and our own currents, which we contribute to this stream. It is so intrinsic to our every moment that, like fish in water, we may fail to see it.

1

The way that can be spoken of is not the eternal Way;
the name that can be named is not the Immortal Name.
Nameless the Source of earth and sky,
names engender every thing.
Unfettered by desire, the mystery reveals itself;
wanting *this* gives rise to *that*.
Beyond named and nameless, reality still flows;
unfathomable the arch, the door, the gate.

YOUR NAME IS A SUMMONS, not a self. Whatever names have been bestowed on you, whatever names you have created for yourself, are only pointers, motes of dust that enable our thoughts to condense and identify an object. But you are not an object; you are a way seeking itself. Names can give the illusion of some unchanging essence "underneath" the name, so don't be deceived; the real you does not stop nor start but swirls and streams.

You are always yourself, moment to moment, in nonstop flow. Your way is not a *becoming* but a *being*, not a matter of now and then, but always: you are the time of your life.

You are not what others think of you; you are not even who you think you are. Thoughts label but do not live. You cannot be summarized in a song, much less captured in a name.

You are not what people call you. Racial slurs and noble honorifics, whether they slander or celebrate you, are mere labels on a garment of identity that is less than skin deep.

Sometimes, angry with yourself, you call yourself names. Sometimes, proud of yourself, you style yourself with sobriquets. You need not deny any part of you, but no single part can stand in for your whole self. You are greater than the sum of your parts, vast in your unique whole-someness.

Feel free to amuse yourself with appellations, but don't feel entitled to your titles or hemmed in by your handles. Affixing labels is just a game of tag. Are you It?

———

After I earned my Ph.D. I worked in clinics as a psychotherapist and neuropsychologist. My clients called me "Doctor," but my internist colleagues were not so certain. I was "Sir" to people wanting to sell me something; "Honey" to my wife, "Dad" to my children, "Bob" to my friends. Taking Buddhist vows, I was given the name Meikyo Onzen ("Clear Mirror Calm Sitting"). Some of my qigong students call me "Teacher."

My daughter attended a ceremony affirming me as a senior student at Berkeley Zen Center. Now, when she sometimes wants advice to fend off, she begins her phone call with an affectionate teasing address: "Oh wise one . . ."

When you call yourself to your Self, do you address yourself that way?

Oh wise one, Dear Reader . . .

2

Point to beauty, then ugly must arise;
distinguishing the good, not-good comes into being.
So this makes that: if life, then death.
If long, then short;
difficult and simple produce each other;
high and low shape each other;
front and back fulfill each other;
first and last subsume each other.
Duets are counterpoints to harmonies.
True people teach without a word;
they are themselves, thus act without exerting effort.
Immersed in flow, no starting and no stopping;
no placing claims, no holding on;
no merit and no fault.

YOUR BEING IS BEAUTIFUL. This beauty does not rely on good looks: beauty rests in being "becoming" to yourself.

Your beauty is unique but nothing special, since beauty is inherent in all existence. If you stand out, your beauty comes in standing out: if you blend in, your beauty comes in blending in. We get confused, though, when we set up relative standards of beauty. We sing "I am pretty" when we feel happy; when we feel unattractive we hope we're ugly ducklings who might later transform into white-plumed

Cygninae or perhaps we take secret pride in the role of a nonconforming black swan.

If you identify with one particular characteristic, you constrict yourself and set the stage for nightmares of its opposite. Investment in appearing lovely invites you to dread losing your looks. If you seek beauty in the fashions of the times you will go in and out of style; if you make up your attractiveness it will wear off.

Beauty is not a commodity; when it is turned into something manufactured, marketed to be bought and sold, it is no longer beauty. Beauty is not something that we own but something that we are: the converging of our pasts and our possibles, presently appearing in a transient form.

All being is absolutely itself. Beauty and ugly are just labels, markers of the whims of personal preference; your true being cannot be captured in such relative concepts. Big and small, pretty and plain, are merely comparisons; when you shift your reference point, your standards shift as well. As Chuang Tzu says:

> From the point of view of differences, if we regard a thing as big because there is a certain bigness to it, then among all the ten thousand things there are none that are not big. If we regard a thing as small because there is a certain smallness to it, then among the ten thousand things there are none that are not small.

Discrimination looks for differences; it finds meaning in contrasts and value in evaluation. Being, though, need not justify itself with meaning. The beauty of being yourself is poetry not prose—the poet Archibald MacLeish advises us that "a poem should not mean, but be." If you're attached to being meaning-full then significance can separate you from connectedness.

Beauty is being fully yourself, without being full of yourself. When you share generously of yourself, you are beautiful. When you know the beauty of yourself as you, then you know the beauty of others as themselves. You allow others to discover themselves in and through you, making no claim on them to be a certain way to satisfy your self-interest. Instead, you discover yourself through the play of being. Self and nonself complete each other, and beauty shimmers.

———

One of my daughters told me she used to be self-conscious of her large nose. Now an adult, she realizes she is quite attractive and her nose contributes to her striking looks. Before she could realize this, though, she confessed her feelings to her boyfriend. From then on, he took care when he embraced her to always kiss her nose first.

A short while ago they married: two noses, four lips, one love.

3

By not giving honors to the worthy
you prevent fights between rivals.
Not prizing anything as a treasure
what have thieves left to steal?
If you don't display objects of desire
minds and hearts are at peace.
Govern by emptying the mind of discrimination
giving the belly what it truly needs;
without straining muscles in willfulness
the bones strengthen in their marrow.
Not knowing "this,"
there is no yearning for "that."
Acting less, harmonizing more
from effortless effort,
order emerges naturally.

YOU ARE A WHOLE PERSON, but you are composed of parts. If you give pride of place to one part over another, though, your parts may not function harmoniously.

Most of us like some parts of ourselves better than others. Some of us are ashamed of our nose, others think their ears are too big. Some pride themselves on their voice, others on their brain. We preen ourselves on our prowess and sulk over our fumbles.

As soon as you set up one part of yourself as better than another, prizing that aspect and disdaining others, you establish the stage for internal conflicts. If you treat your volunteering at a local homeless shelter as virtuous, when you feel tired and want to spend a quiet evening at home you may regard your natural needs as "selfish" and feel unworthy. Each, though, has its time and place.

Why do you tie yourself into knots between "should" and "shouldn't?" Your heart pumps blood throughout your body without picking and choosing; every cell gets its fair share of oxygen whether it be in your noble eyes or stinking feet. If you allocated your blood according to what parts of you are desirable, neuropathy would soon set in.

Attention is the mind's gift to self and world both. When you are free from excessive desire the beam of your attention widens and it can clarify wherever it alights. When your interior landscape and the territory right in front of you are both illuminated, action comes naturally without unnecessary striving. You discover whatever is necessary to meet the call of the moment: now this, now that.

——

After some years of doing qigong I discovered my tastes were changing. Perhaps it was just part of normal aging, but it seemed that as my body and mind became more coordinated and naturally healthy, I started to learn what was truly satisfying. As I stopped fighting with myself over "bad" food cravings (ice cream! chips! doughnuts!) or telling myself what I "should" eat, fruits and vegetables became genuine treats.

Sometimes, though, when life is difficult, there is no shame in an occasional bag of Doritos. Without the internal struggle, there is neither overindulgence nor skimping, no surfeit and no lack.

4

The Tao is empty, meaning free;
endless, beginningless like a circle,
inexhaustible, the source and ancestor of all—
it rounds our edges, unties our tangles,
softens our light, settles the dust—
clear beyond clear, dark beyond dark,
presents itself
whose child it is, being
as it is before Before.

You are a living organism, not some thing. Being no-thing, you must make friends with emptiness.

Emptiness is not a void: it is an inexhaustible well of possibilities and connectedness. When you empty yourself out by letting go of your need to make something of yourself, you free yourself: you can then be reborn as your actual self, the child being parent to the woman or man.

Whose child are you? Whoever your parents were, portions of their "who" consisted of who their parents were, and so on for your grandmothers and grandfathers and all the prior generations. The parents of our parents' parents' parents many times removed would have been members of some other species, and that species descended from another species, and so on back to when life arose through an assembly of compounds. Those compounds were themselves assemblies of elements; elements assemblies of atoms; atoms assemblies of quarks.

I read recently that Australian researchers have determined sea sponges and humans share genes and a common ancestor. Like sponges, you and I are assemblies of cells and organs, molecules and minds, *p*s and *q*s and *me*s and *you*s. Are we just these bits and pieces? On the other hand, if we are not made up of our separate parts, what are we?

This is the wrong question. You and I are not *what*s; our *who*s are made up of our *where*s and *when*s. Even that formulation can be misleading since it implies "where" and "when" are concrete immutables. Your "where," though, is a tectonically unstable spinning globe perpetually hurtling through space; you can travel, but never grasp, this flowing conveyance. Your "when" is ungraspable not only as history but even as a present moment.

We are all the children of our history; without it we would not exist. That history, though, cannot be touched, tasted, smelled, seen, or pinned down to a limited set of facts. Your history is constantly changing as you continue to live. Not only do you change as you encounter new experiences, but neuropsychological research shows your memories of your past are inaccurate. Every time we remember something, we alter it: we do not retrieve traces of the past but reconstruct our history anew each time we call it up.

Because your history is ungraspable, so is your self. Because it is ungraspable, it is "empty": it does not contain hard edges of immutable characteristics. The river stone comes from the mountain's bone: tossed up against other stones by the swirling currents of the stream, its edges are ground away, and it becomes beautiful in its smooth roundness.

———

I devoted about a year in meditation to attempting to "be in the moment." I failed.

Try it: you'll find as soon as you say "this moment" it has already passed you by. This has profound repercussions.

The Diamond Sutra points out not only is the past gone and the future not yet here, but *the present cannot be grasped.* So what time do you exist in?

You don't pass through time. You *are* time, Being.

5

Heaven and earth do not center on humans;
they treat all things impartially,
unmoved by wishes and pleas.
The true person is not a humanist
but is clear as heaven, common as dirt.
Heaven and earth move like a bellows,
empty yet never depleted,
resounding with each movement.
Words exhaust meaning;
just center on centering.

YOU ARE THE CENTER of the universe, but don't be misled: each person is the center of the universe. In fact every being, each particle, is the center of the universe.

How can this be so? You are not the center of your remote inaccessible universe and your friends are not the centers of their particular secluded universes. That would make for zillions of isolated galaxies when in reality all galaxies are related to each other in the gravity of their being. The universe includes everything, and from every point in it you can see it is constantly expanding.

Centers are not locations but sources of light. In this way, all centers touch the Center. Though disparate in place and time, form and function, each center is alike in its centeredness: a moment of balance.

The center of your being is a vector of all the forces concentrated on the point of your existence. You cannot put your finger on it (the very act of trying to do so will alter it), but you can sense your center. Being yourself is finding your balance by returning to your center again and again.

The universe does not discriminate between centers. The universe does not care about you in particular, nor do humans occupy a privileged place; the universe moves along its Way, following its laws. Whether you are a man or a woman, young or old, you are a natural living being. So is a dog. So is a rock. So is the flowing ocean and the still pond. Each being is a central expression of Being. Gravity and light, space and time treat each alike.

Your vantage point, though, is uniquely your own and, while it may be central, it is also inherently limited. When it rains, the rain falls on everyone and everything equally, but you may see it as a hindrance to your vacation plans while a cactus sees it as a signal to blossom.

Humans are a very small part of the cosmos. If you let the human get in the way of what is natural, you oppose yourself to the entirety of the universe. This takes a great deal of work: control of nature requires constant effort and, in the long view (which is the only view the universe entertains, an eyeblink or a billion years), it is doomed to fail.

Still, the cosmos is the integral stuff that composes us and all being. So just be composed. Being natural, you need not worry about becoming yourself: just pour yourself out and do that which is truly becoming to all the matrices of the moment. Then you blossom fully as a part of the vast matrix, as one center of the universe, and express your place in the scheme of things.

———

The first Zen meditation retreat I went to was in the early 1970s, a time of a reawakening of feminist models of relationship and a reimagining of gender roles. One woman was concerned about the patriarchal traditions of Zen and asked the Zen teacher how this might affect meditation.

The teacher suggested, "When you meditate, go to a place where you are neither man nor woman, so you can come back and be truly man, truly woman."

This is not a matter of hetero or homo, transgender, bisexual, macho or butch, domination or submission, repletion or depletion. It is beyond reproduction but is at the center of intercourse.

The in and out of a breathing bellows, the rhythm of love expressed, heaven meeting earth in a kiss: this is how something comes from nothing. It is the love in which you lose yourself to find yourself.

6

The valley spirit is deathless:
the unborn womb,
the door,
the root of heaven and earth,
the Source,
subtly everlasting
beyond existence and nonexistence.
Constantly we draw on it;
it graces us by being inexhaustible.

PERHAPS YOU DO NOT want to die; perhaps you even wish to be immortal. Be advised: eternity not only never dies but is originally unborn. This is true for all being: that which gives life to life is not itself alive; that which brings death can never die.

You may not know how to live, but so long as you are alive, you will live. You may not know how to die, but—as I once heard a Tibetan teacher say—"Don't worry about dying . . . you'll be able to do it."

The key to being truly yourself is to be free from fear. Don't fear dying; don't fear living. To be free from fear, though, you must know what you can really rely on.

What can you truly rely on? You cannot rely on your abilities: muscles weaken, organs fail, memories fade. Consciousness floats in and out on a momentary basis. We cannot rely on being always awake, and we cannot count on being always asleep even when we die, for nobody knows what death entails.

If we cannot rely even on ourselves, how can we possibly rely on others? Even those who love us most dearly will sometimes be tired or unavailable; even with the best of will they cannot provide precisely what we want whenever we want it. We often cannot even be clear about what we want or need. Our desire for someone else to know and fulfill our needs is as human as the child's desire to be taken care of by the parent and just as fated to be fraught with failures of empathy, perceived intrusions, and unavoidable abandonments.

Earth underlies all and the firmament soars above all. Still, you cannot rely on earth to be the way you want it: sinkholes settle and volcanoes erupt, soil washes away. Earth is always underfoot, but sometimes it may be a forest floor, other times quicksand—and in any case, we humans have a tendency to cover it with concrete. The sky is always overhead, but sunshine and rain will come and go regardless of your desires for the day.

You cannot rely on any particular weather forecast, but you can rely on there always being some kind of weather. You cannot rely on any particular phenomenon, but you can be sure that phenomena will appear and disappear. You cannot rely on the earth being a particular way, but the physicality of matter and the dynamics of energy continue their expressive conversations. The sky may change its appearance, but whether you see clouds or not, the stars are always there, though even they are constantly changing.

You cannot rely on your beliefs: these are a matter of ideology. Beliefs can be tested and sometimes found wanting; clinging to beliefs can lead to disappointment or zealotry. You can, however, keep the faith if you rely on what is true: beyond words and understanding, life-and-death goes on, inexhaustible, gracing us with the currency of unceasing flow.

Something emerges mysteriously from nothing, sound rests eternally on silence. When the lake dries up, the meadow will appear. When the meadow is filled with trees, the birds will nest. When the forests are consumed with flames, the pinecones will release their seeds.

———

I was hiking over a pass in Ladakh at around seventeen thousand feet when my legs suddenly lost sensation and stopped responding to my brain's instructions. My companion had to leave me for an hour to obtain help. During this time I sat and looked across the empty high desert plain and, knowing I was suffering from a stroke, complained to the mountain peaks: "I might die here, now, alone!"

The mountains looked back at me and in their silent way answered: "So? What's so special? We, too, live and die."

This was very comforting. My fear melted, giving way to feelings of belonging and compassion.

7

Heaven endures forever, earth lasts eternally,
because they do not live for themselves.
Heaven covers everything equally, earth upholds all,
so they are immortal.
Thus the True Person does not put herself forward.
Leaving self behind is at the forefront;
this safeguards true self.
Since you are not It, but It actually is you,
you meet yourself everywhere
and are completely fulfilled every when.

BEING YOURSELF doesn't mean being selfish. When we think only of ourselves we create a split in ourselves; there is the part doing the thinking and the part we are thinking about. When we become divided in ourselves with an anxious self-consciousness, we tend to stumble.

Athletes know this. If you try to do a somersault off a high diving board by telling yourself to approach the edge with strides fourteen inches long, to bend your knees at a 110-degree angle and push off your feet with ten pounds of force, you're likely to wind up in a belly flop or body cast. Abandon yourself to the spring of the plank beneath your feet, to your body's expression of gravity falling to the water waiting below, and you'll make less of a splash.

Many of our difficulties come from our desire to make a big splash.

This is a romantic misunderstanding of the sources of creativity. Creativity is a gift, not a self-inflation. Where do ideas come from? Artists speak reverently of the grace of some inspiration beyond themselves; as vehicles for their muse, they seek to express the inexpressible.

We have a human tendency to hold on, to become attached: we invest our sense of ourselves in the outcome of what we do. If we are excessively selfish, though, we become defensive and rigid: our undivided activity breaks down in a separation of actor and object, and what was playful begins to take a lot of effort. Art becomes artsy when ego asserts its dominance over creation.

If we only pursue our own interests, aiming at ourselves we narrow our field of action. Then being yourself ceases to be a good-natured romp and instead becomes hard work, a struggle between "mine" and "yours"; we strain caught in the illusions of "success" and "failure."

The solution is easy: when you don't get in the way of the Way, you find fulfillment because "empty" self is connected self, meeting in a moment. Opening yourself to whatever is right in front of you, you recognize yourself in everything.

Treating everything as ourselves, living not for ourselves but as a true person who covers everything and upholds all, a vast field opens transparent throughout. We are not the world: the world is us.

———

Leaving Nanda Devi basin, hiking south from Martoli, the trail winds for miles several hundred feet above the river Gori. At thirty-three hundred meters, the sky is a crisp blue and the only sound to compete with the rivers' rushing is the occasional bleat from mountain sheep. The sound of the river became the susurration of the blood surging through my arteries and veins.

On this exploratory trek in the Indian Himalaya with my friend Joel, we used a team of horsemen to carry our gear. Their most junior member, Biru, swore to being eighteen but was probably closer to fourteen, judging by his boyish antics. He had just tagged along from the village with the head horseman, but he put in more work than the others and we all adopted him as an unofficial member of our group.

One day I was the last to leave our campsite, but felt rested and fit and soon caught up to the horsemen. Mischievous Biru, however, decided to play a game of catch-up. Whenever I got close to overtaking him, he whipped the mule to make it go faster and stay one step ahead of me. He'd look back at me, his smiling eyes would make contact with mine, and we'd meet each other in laughter.

During this trip Joel was mourning his brother who had died a short time ago. Shortly after Biru and I finished our game, our group crossed a plank bridge and a black dog with a brown muzzle, who had befriended us and followed us for days, reached the boundary of his territory. When the dog sat on his haunches and howled we all felt the pain of parting.

Three years earlier Joel and I had hiked hundreds of miles away on the shores of lake Tso Moriri at fifteen thousand feet in Ladakh; the lake is sacred to the Chang-pa herdsmen, who live as nomads in the surrounding high desert plains. I paused to erect a cairn, dedicating each stone to one of the people I loved back home so their spirits could mingle with the lake's. We stopped to visit a remote school that houses the children of the nomads during their parents' wanderings and this saying greeted us on its gate: "Others Before Self."

8

Truly good people are like water,
bringing help to all without picking and choosing.
Not contending, not striving, not competing,
going places others avoid, flowing like the Way,
rooted in earth, minds like deep pools,
helping with kindness, speaking with sincerity,
governing with peace, working with skill, moving with time.
No contention, no fault.

YOU AND I are not opposed to one another. Life is not necessarily a zero-sum game where if you have more, I'll have less. This is a fiction based on a narrow vision that pits self and others against one another. In reality, we are all in this together.

When there is enough to share, there is no problem. When there is not enough to share, if everyone goes out foraging there will be more. Even when you are on a seesaw and it looks like one is up and the other is down, each relies on the other in a balancing relationship and the individual positions are merely temporary.

Capitalism glorifies competition, but being yourself is no contest. You are unique. Problems only arise when we compare our relative worth to others'. If you think of some people as being good, there is nobody who does not have some goodness about them. If you think of some people as being bad, there is nobody that does not have some badness.

As soon as you start making comparisons you open a door for self-doubt: where do you belong on the measurement scale? We are used to worrying about whether we're "normal," but normality did not even exist until people gathered in urban centers and statisticians began to tabulate how they were distributed. Once the normal curve was constructed, people were placed relative to the mean.

It's not possible to have a normal curve where all the children are "above average," some must be below for others to be above. So instead of each student simply being who she is, grades are assigned. When society tries to put people in their "proper" place, everyone struggles with their position on the totem pole.

Life is not fundamentally something to contend with but something to explore and appreciate. You appreciate it by contributing to it as yourself. Your self is not a measured thing but a streaming flow of relationships with people, with living beings, and with the material world that surrounds you and holds you.

Dwell with earth; think with depth; help with kindness. It's easy to be sincere when you stop pretending to be anything other than who you are. There's no place for blame when your skill consists of simply being yourself, a word spoken in time, flowing still.

———

The ability to let go of contentious argument sometimes lets deeper wellsprings of sincerity emerge. In my first job after graduating high school, I worked as an office boy. It was 1968, and the Vietnam War had polarized the country into "longhairs" and "hardhats," "peaceniks" and "patriots." My hair was a little long, and I opposed the war. One of my fellow office workers, a man much older than me, was a self-identified Nixon voter and supporter of the war. He ragged me incessantly about being a "hippy-commie-pinko." Yet when I quit work to go to college, he was the only one who gave me a gift.

I remember he was somewhat embarrassed when he gave me my present, muttering something about how he didn't know what I would like, so he'd tried his best to figure out what a college-bound eighteen-year-old would want. When I later opened up his present I found a book of poetry by Ho Chi Minh, the leader of the North Vietnamese in the war. My seeming antagonist had reached beyond his own views and preferences to wish me well on what he felt were my own terms.

How kind of him. I have never forgotten him.

9

Pouring more and more into a vessel?
Better to stop in time.
Honing and honing a blade?
Its sharp edge will not last.
Fill a house with treasure, it will never be safe.
Rich, exalted, and proud, you invite blame and failure.
When the work is done, stop: retire and rest.
This is the Way of heaven.

MORE IS NOT BETTER. Sometimes more can be the enemy of enough; when an amount is just right, anything more than enough is extra.

Moving with time requires knowing when to stop in time. If a plumber tightens the pipe connection too much, it will leak. An excess of spice overwhelms all other tastes; if you try too hard to realize yourself, you will become artificially flavored. Overextend yourself, and muscles and mind contract.

Steering free of pride, knowing there is nothing to be ashamed of, you open to yourself in all being, and find there's plenty of room. *Just this* is self-sufficiency.

When I worked in a large medical center I often saw physicians reach for a prescription pad in an effort to do something for a patient quickly; they did not feel comfortable "just" listening to their patients, despite knowing that simply feeling heard was often more healing for a patient than a medication or invasive procedure. I came to realize I, too, am often prone to offer a "fix" to people I love when I see them suffering. I want to do more to help them and find it difficult to just stop, offer myself as a witness, and trust the present of my presence is enough.

Similarly when I encounter a difficulty I work harder at solving the problem. Sometimes this is helpful but sometimes it's just stubbornness—refusing to acknowledge that when you're stuck in snow pressing the car's accelerator and spinning the wheels only digs you in deeper. This caused me a lot of suffering in the early years of my Zen practice. I poured more and more of myself into zazen, but this only led me to feel worse and worse.

One day I confided my difficulties to a friend and a senior practitioner at Berkeley Zen Center, Maylie Scott. I was surprised when she said, "maybe you should do less zazen, or maybe even not do any for a little while."

This was a tremendous gift. It eased the pressure and I found that once I let up I didn't need to stop zazen, I only needed to stop "doing" zazen and let the sitting settle into itself. It's like drawing a circle: when you let go of trying to draw a perfectly smooth line you find you can rely, instead, on roundness.

I still get stuck sometimes. When I do, I find it helps to stop pushing and go wider. Some words from Maylie's Metta Prayer help remind me:

> May I be at ease in my body, feeling the ground beneath my seat and feet . . .
> May I be attentive and gentle toward my own discomfort and suffering . . .
> May I be attentive and grateful for my own joy and well-being . . .
> May I move toward others freely and with openness . . .
> May I receive others with sympathy and understanding.

10

While carrying on your active life,
can you embrace the quiet spirit in your arms
without letting it wander away?
While being fully focused on your breath,
can you let it be soft as a baby's?
In cleaning your inner mirror,
can you wipe it free of dust?
At the opening and closing of heaven's gate,
can you be like a mother bird?
In loving people,
can you lead without imposing your will?
Can you govern all states without effort?
Being enlightened, comprehending all—
can you light up the world without knowing anything special?
Give birth, nurture—but don't claim you own them.
Protect and keep them, but don't possess them.
Cultivating, growing, not self-centered controlling—
this is fathomless virtue, beyond light and dark.

LIVING REQUIRES EFFORT. *How* you exert yourself, though, is more important than *how much* you exert yourself. If you don't exert yourself, you will never stretch beyond your current boundaries, but if you exert yourself by forcing and straining, there's a good chance you'll break down or cause harm.

Sometimes you may feel tired and need to rest; sometimes you may feel tired and need to persevere. Sometimes when we feel pain it is a signal that continuing on will cause injury; other times the pain we experience is a phantasm caused more by anxiety than by any actual physical threat. This also applies to efforts of the mind: pushing yourself to work on a task when you feel you've reached your limits may result in a breakthrough or may lead to errors and exhaustion.

The same is true of heartfelt feelings. Perhaps you're falling in love with someone and experiencing more and more intimacy but also more and more fear, sadness, and even anger. Are you dealing with old patterns you need to confront so you can reach deeper levels of connection in this relationship or are these feelings signals that you need to extricate yourself from an unhealthy relationship pattern?

Which signals do you listen to, and which do you need to override? When should you put forth more effort, and when should you let go? To answer these questions you must know yourself well. To know yourself well, you need to let go of the ideas you have about yourself and be sensitive to how you actually respond.

When you do this, life will teach you what you need to know. If you put forth too much effort in a physical task, you will get injuries beyond the normal soreness that lasts a day or two. If you put forth too little, you will plateau and not strengthen or grow. If you put too much energy into a relationship that is not reciprocated, you will become depressed and/or angry; too little and you will feel guilty or unsatisfied.

At any particular choice point, you cannot know the answer beforehand: if you could it would be a selection, not a choice. When faced with a range of possible paths, you can never know how your choice will turn out. No matter how much information you collect, no matter how carefully you map out contingencies, you cannot foresee all the eddies that will result from your actions until you actually undertake them. Each time you commit yourself to a course of action, you plunge into unpredictability because the results are not dependent only on your efforts but on the reactions of all around you, spreading like ripples through the world.

Because of this, it helps to leaven all your choices with compassion.

Choices are children: you don't own them, but you can take responsibility for nurturing them. If you try to control what happens purely for the sake of your own interests, you narrow the field; if you cultivate whatever emerges, you can prepare to be surprised.

We live in the darkness of unknowing, certain of uncertainty crowning the present, doubting the rest. Still, the night is full of stars. Knowing you don't know what will happen, act wholeheartedly. See what happens, then respond. When you let go of imposing your will, the onus of obligation dissolves and gives way to the joy of response-ability: cultivating the own-being of all you encounter along your way.

———

One of my college professors, Taitetsu Unno, said to our small group at the end of our time together: "My wish for you," he said, "is that you may live each moment of your life with full effort, each moment 100 percent. Not 90 percent. Also not 110 percent."

I had always fended off criticism and failure by showing others (and myself) that I was straining with all my might: I assumed that, in all things, more effort was better. The idea that it might not be was a revelation to me.

Around the same time I started learning meditation. It would take me a while to figure out that meditation is not anything special. Meditation is not a matter of controlling your mind but of doing no more and no less than is needed at any moment.

The same is true of physical effort. Most of us know that if you tense up to control your golf swing the ball will slice, that if you over-swing at a fastball you'll strike out. It's not necessarily easy, though, to let go of being willful and learn to be willing: to trust ourselves to flow with whatever is needed without falling into over- or under-doing.

I've found the moving meditation of Dayan Qigong helpful for learning something of the knack of surrendering to full-hearted *wu wei*, "effortless effort." Throughout the sixty-four movements of Dayan Qigong we let our hands open, fingers extended and spread, relaxed but vital, with the palm cupped just enough to cultivate energy and health so that we can nurture ourselves and others. Open hands, open heart.

11

Thirty spokes converge on one hub;
the center is empty, so the wheel can turn.
A pot is made from clay;
the center is empty, so the vessel can be used.
Windows and doors are cut for a house;
the center is empty, so there's room to live.
The being of a thing makes it handy;
its nonbeing lets it function.

CENTERS ARE NOT SETTLEMENTS but moments of being. To put forth just the right kind of effort you need to act from the center of your being—then all parts of you function in concert and you don't exhaust yourself.

Even in simple actions such as standing or sitting, the more balanced you are around your center, the less muscle strain you will experience and the more easily you will be able to maintain your stance. This holds true for mental stances and efforts as much as for physical ones.

It is easy to become confused and imagine our center has some substance to it. We believe that we have a stable personal identity; we fashion an image of who we think we are or who we want to be and then try to adhere to that image. We hope to balance our bodies to achieve some eternal equilibrium and pray to pacify our minds to attain everlasting inner peace. Our physical centers, though, do not reside permanently in some specific part of our body, nor do our mind centers have some stable trait or core content that constitutes the essence of ourselves. The world is always changing and, since we are not separate from the world, we are always changing.

So we have this problem: how can we be consistently ourselves yet constantly changing? Actually, this is not a problem, just the reality that our lives are flowing. When we resist this flow by attaching ourselves to a fixed image, we take that which is ungraspable and make it into a thing. We halt our living truth for the sake of a convenient handle; we put a dent in our true selves and become attached to I-dent-ities.

Your center is dynamic. Your physical center of gravity changes depending on your posture and position: it is a vector, the result of all the different forces acting within and upon you at a given moment. When you breathe only with the upper portion of your lungs, your center of gravity goes up along with the tension in your shoulders; when you relax your breath and breathe from your diaphragm, your physical center lowers.

This is good news. It means you can alter your physical center of gravity through being aware of it. The more you relax, the more stable your center of gravity becomes and the less effort you need to expend.

The same holds true for your emotional, mental, and spiritual well-being. The more tightly you hold on to certain ideas about yourself, the more they get in the way of realizing who you are at this particular moment. Fortunately, though, since the hub is empty, nothing gets in the way of being you.

When we hear "the center is empty," we may feel anxiety. If there is no "core" to me, who am I? But in reality the opposite holds true: if there is a "core" to me, it can be damaged or lost. When your core is an ever-shifting vector of all the forces within and without, all the experiences you have had, are currently having, and might have, you become a shimmering of dynamic possibilities.

In mathematics, points are dimensionless in and of themselves: they exist only as intersections. Emptiness is just such a turning point, the pivot of our lives.

My mid-fifties brought many changes. Our children had grown and my wife of thirty years had left me. My employer was no longer allowing us to perform our clinical work the way we wanted to. I sought solace hiking the mountains, but a stroke ended my trek.

When I returned home I was bereft of all my badges of identity. I could not function as a neuropsychologist, since I was unable to perform the very tests I was supposed to administer to my patients. My poststroke physical and mental problems made it difficult to do qigong. My reliance on Zen meditation had been shaken when, facing possible death in the mountains, I found myself doing a *metta*, or loving-kindness, meditation more characteristic of the Vipassana tradition than of Zen.

So there I was: not a husband, not an active parent, not a neuropsychologist, not a qigong teacher, and even my meditation practice was not what I thought it "should" be. Losing all my roles and everything I identified as "me" was painful. I could not feel, at the time, the liberation it offered, how it would prove to be the pivot point allowing me to unearth the foundations of my life, the true means by which I live.

Over the next year, forced to go to the empty hub of my being, in losing myself I'd find myself.

12

Five colors blind our seeing.
Five notes deafen our hearing.
Five flavors blunt our palate.
Hunting and racing hurry us, madden us.
Hard-to-get goods tempt us to break our journey.
Sage governing
satisfies the hungry belly's need, not the eye's hunger,
leaves that illusion, plunges into *just this.*

THE WORLD CAN APPEAR very convincing. Don't be deceived.

Although we think what we see, hear, and feel is reality, at best it is a small window; at worst it is a distorting filter. All of our perceptions are colored and filtered by our senses and the language we use to get a handle on our ungraspable experience.

The colors of the rainbow are not seven: Newton named them ROYGBIV when he broke light into a spectrum through his prisms because he arbitrarily wanted the number of hues to match the number of notes in a musical scale. Rainbows' colors are infinite, but their names depend on what language you speak; for example, some languages predispose their speakers to name blue and green as shades of the same hue.

Rainbows' colors extend beyond the realm of human perception: our eyes cannot perceive the ultraviolet and infrared wavelengths of light. The thought "the sky is blue" can mislead us to a false sense of constancy, forgetting the magenta of sunsets and the electric silver of thunderstorms, the ebony of starry nights and the shocking greens of the aurora borealis.

We are rarely aware of how many mundane messages are constantly bombarding us, each broadcasting a version of "reality." Walking down the street, the clothes you see others wearing, the thermometers posted on bank signs, and the numbers shown on television weather broadcasts tell you how warm or cool you "should" be feeling regardless of your personal temperature. Perhaps when you were growing up and pushed aside some of the food on your plate, your parents discouraged your faith in your own taste by saying "you don't know what's good for you." As adults in a consumer society, your wants are not your own: you are always being told what you should desire. Billboards say "buy this," ballads sing "feel that," reinforcing your anxiety that you should be hunting for more goods, more sensations, and more satisfaction.

These messages deliver only the appearance of reality, not reality itself. They encourage desires that feel urgent when in truth they are transient mirages: pursuing them will not lead to contentment.

We know what it means to be truly satisfied but we get distracted and forget to listen closely to our true selves. Satisfaction, like reality itself, is not something you can grasp; you find it not in the lusts of the eye nor the admonishments of advertisements but in the deeper darker wisdom of your guts and the visceral mine of your heart-mind's being.

Satisfaction is simply realizing who you are in the warp and weave of here and now. There is no need to look further away than to ask yourself: how can I find fulfillment and appreciate what is right before me this moment?

———

Driving in the Skagit Valley of the Pacific Northwest, after the rain, good weather—the sun shone through the remnants of mist and a perfect double rainbow appeared immediately off the road to our right. Not fifty yards away it seemed to hover tangibly just a few feet above the ground; my lover and I saw the end of the rainbow beckoning to us, sparkling on the flat farmland, turning it to gold.

We pulled off the road, stopped the car, and tried to walk somewhere over the rainbow. But the pot of treasure at the end eluded us; the closer we got to it the more it receded until we stopped and, looking at each other, realized ourselves in light. The sun and rain bathed not just land and air in gold but ourselves as well.

13

Honor, disgrace—watch out!
Disaster, great misfortune—respect them as the body!
Honor and disgrace are like warnings
because they elevate and depress us.
Gaining and losing are two forms of bondage.
Disaster, great misfortune—these bring distress.
The body is the seat of distress; no body, no distress
so treasure the body as the world.
Body in the world, world in the body.
Loving mutuality,
true entrustment.

SUCCESS IS OVERRATED. We reach for accomplishment thinking it will bolster our sense of ourselves, but success is often short-lived, usually circumscribed to a narrow sphere, and always subject to the slippages and pressures of our personal plate tectonics.

As soon as we conceive of success we inevitably engender the possibility of failure. Nobody is successful all the time and even when you are successful, it is easy to feel anxious ("Will I be able to sustain this? What will they want next?") or to denigrate your abilities as not "really" anything special ("Aw, shucks . . ."). Whatever your abilities may be, they are neither ordinary nor special: they're simply unique to you.

We are elated when we are praised, sad or angry when we are punished. Success and failure, ways the world measures your value, are twin chimeras because your self is immeasurable: self is not a thing that can be valued like merchandise in a store. Your salary reflects socioeconomics, not selfhood. Praise and punishment are ways parents control children: being yourself requires growing up.

Whether it is others or your own internal critic who is awarding plaudits and subtracting demerits, it is not easy to break free of success and failure. Our behavior is shaped by reinforcements positive and negative. When disaster strikes, though—when everything is taken away from us except life itself—we find our foundation not in the ups and downs of outrageous fortune but in existence itself. Our senses may be deprived of calm, our mind stricken with pain, but our breath still flows. We continuously embody our life, through honor and disgrace alike.

Fully embodied as yourself, you find you and the world are connected. The soil is not only under your feet but in your body: iron in your blood, minerals in your organs. Rub against the world and your skin sloughs off, contributing its constituents to the dust around you so that you are represented in the lands you touch. Your breath is an exchange with the world, your actions are interactions anchored in gravity and made possible by the frictions of feeling.

Your body does not belong to you: you belong to your body, which is the whole world. You are not it: it actually is you.

—

My kindergarten teacher sat at the front of the room reading from a book seemingly several feet tall. She'd point to a word then point to one of us to pronounce it. The print on the page was a mystery to me; I always failed. I feared school.

In first grade I had an epiphany: words were sounds. Suddenly I could read any book placed before me. My teacher praised me inordinately; she gave me more and more difficult books until she had me performing in front of sixth grade classes, reading their books out loud to them. There was only one problem: I didn't understand what I was reading.

I could not let go of the kudos that came my way for being so "advanced," but inwardly I felt uncomprehending, awkward, and scared. Surely some day my pretense would be discovered and I would be unmasked as a fraud. The outward show and the inward insecurity manifested in my body: I was awkward and poorly coordinated. I had many bouts of pneumonia and bronchitis, and I frequently felt depressed.

The discrepancy between outward show and inner experience came to a climax during college. I majored in music composition but at a certain point had to confront my lack of talent. I failed a physics course; my girlfriend left me; I fell apart.

Fortunately in the midst of this I took a gym class in hatha yoga, and was taught that *yoga* means *union*. I learned to breathe deeply and let the breath move the body into various positions, experiencing sensations in muscles I never even knew I had. I realized I didn't know my body, and this ignorance was more significant than my lack of mastery of musical chords, physics, and the mysteries of college mixers.

It was a relief to finally acknowledge my distress, to begin learning to treasure this aching body and this confused mind, and to recognize that the very gap between ignorance and understanding is what calls for trust and enables exploration. Self and world, mind and body, delusion and enlightenment call to each other in loving mutuality.

14

It cannot be seen, so we name it unclear;
it cannot be heard, so we name it indistinct;
it cannot be grasped, so we name it insubstantial.
Incomprehensible: warp and weft of the One.
Beyond light and dark, beyond up and down,
beyond here and there, neither formless nor formed,
it cannot be named.
Waxing and waning, re-turning itself,
its empty vast no-thing original face.
Endless beginning!
Not before nor behind, every where It greets us,
every when meeting It,
we meet ourselves meeting,
thread the tread of this Way.

BECAUSE THE WAY cannot be seen, heard, smelled, or grasped, we sometimes have trouble staying in touch with it. This is particularly true when the universe feels cruel and wrong.

Everyone knows the pain of innocence betrayed. Some of us have experienced this more intensely than others, but nobody gets through life without knowing the misery of reaching out for comfort and security and being greeted instead by a tsunami of hurt and loss. Nature's earthquakes kill hundreds of thousands in a few seconds; humanity's wars enlist children to join in massacres. You are hungry and your parent does not feed you; you are lonely and your lover does not embrace you; you are ill and the physician cannot take away your pain. At such times, when you reach out, what can you rely on?

Buddhist practitioners like to say we are like a person who, pursued by a tiger to the edge of a tall cliff, clambers down a few feet to escape the tiger's claws and hangs on to a small bush for dear life. The tiger crouches above, swiping at its prey, the roots of the bush are starting to pull out, and there is a long drop below. The bush has a single strawberry on it; if you pluck it and pop it into your mouth, its sweetness will permeate you completely.

Or not. Sometimes the bush bears no strawberry but only thorns. All that is left is the fierceness of the sun beating down, the hot breath of the tiger above, and the cold wind sweeping up from below. What then?

Any object you look to can abandon you; any plea can fall on deaf ears; any lifeboat can be tossed by waves and slip from your grasp. Anything outside yourself can die, disappear, or not be there when you need it. Inside yourself the geography is not any more stable. Although you may have been taught to be self-reliant, like everyone else you sometimes fail both others and yourself.

When we feel abandoned and alone, when the universe is too vast, the world too much with us, sometimes we call it despair, sometimes we label it a hollow darkness: sometimes we complain, "I feel so empty." The emptiness that can be named, though, is not true emptiness: it is mere desolation, a presence of an absence, a vacuity: it is a relative darkness that grieves for the missing light.

All these kinds of "emptiness" are not true emptiness: they have definable negative qualities. Fortunately, though, the emptiness that is at our heart has no defining characteristics: it is fluid and ungraspable. Being ungraspable, it is limitless, a timeless refuge for us and all being.

If a refuge is a walled-off sanctuary, it can be breached; when the refuge expands to include all that is, was, and ever will be, there are no gaps. If your heart were full, holding on to its vital fluid, it could not let the old blood in nor allow the new blood, rich in oxygen, to move out to every cell in your body. Your heart, when it is fully open, beats continuously; its circulation is a circle without beginning or end, an oscillating *lub-dub* vast as the pulsing of Being itself.

To know yourself fully is to know your place in this vastness, but the vastness cannot be seen, heard, felt, or smelled; it cannot be touched by any of the senses. Still, it is there. Getting out of bed in the morning after your child has been murdered, when all your hopes are dead, requires an act of faith—the faith that remains when all your beliefs have shattered.

Fortunately, the impulse to wake up comes from somewhere beyond yourself. It is as intimate as opening your eyes, throwing off the warm covers of your sleep, and taking one step and then another. Each step and each breath is a rebirth of trust.

This may seem incomprehensible in the face of the hurts of the world. It is impossible. It is continuously real nonetheless.

———

I woke up after a disturbed night's sleep of earthquakes and executions. It was time to get up for morning meditation but it was hard to get out of bed. It was cold and dark, the bed was warm and beckoning, the body said, "you need more sleep," the mind felt sluggish and depressed.

I struggled to rouse myself but found myself snuggling deeper under the blankets. I resolved to count down from ten to one and then throw off the covers, but somewhere around the number four I slowed down and by two the willpower was gone.

Finally I gave up. I acknowledged I was unable to rouse myself and prepared to sleep in.

The next thing I knew, I was standing up out of bed, putting on my clothes. I had no idea how this happened. It seemed as mysterious as waking up itself.

What wakes us up in truth? When *this* greets you, you are face to face with yourself.

15

Your beginningless ancestors, skilled at sounding
the mysteries of the unfathomable Way,
appear deeply ordinary, profoundly unremarkable.
Not standing out, merged with continuous practice,
not recognizable, I describe them with reluctance.
Careful, like crossing rivers in winter,
mindful of neighbors, respectful as a guest,
ephemeral as melting ice,
simple as uncarved wood,
broad and open as a valley.
Muddy water in transparent glass
clarifies itself in stillness.
At the center of stillness, arousing to life.
As you treasure this Way
there's no urge for excess fulfillment,
so you'll not be worn out, but always renewed.

THE SOIL OF OURSELVES is very ordinary: bits of protein and lipids, flashes of thoughts and perceptions across synapses, fluid feelings and impulses running through our relationships. Whenever a fragment of ourselves comes to the forefront of our conscious ego, it wants to run the show or at least stir up some lively action. But emotions and notions, judgments and desires are temporary visitors in the larger ecology of yourself. When we forget this we lose our freedom.

You have the freedom to walk across any river in winter, but if the ice is thin you will break through. You have the freedom to break an intimate silence with your lover, but words may shatter the mood. You can express all your desires to the people around you, but you might be advised to choose a good time and place for your requests and to consider negotiating rather than demanding. You have the freedom to tell your boss off, so long as you are willing to lose your job and go hungry.

Limits and liberty can be friends; wisdom lies in reconciling restrictions with possibilities. We live on a continuously round earth under an inexhaustible vast sky, but we are anchored in the gritty reality that soil needs conservation or, overused, becomes dust blown to the winds. Liberation is freedom from hindrances: being an absence, it cannot be grasped, so it need not celebrate itself only in loud leaps but also in the unremarkable ability to quietly move forward or back. Like the coastline of Great Britain, which can be shown mathematically to be infinitely long yet enclose a finite area, liberation's endless horizons rest on constraint. It behooves us to be careful.

We don't always want to be careful. We are easily stirred up; especially when we strive to be extraordinary, our passions can run high. We fear our failures will scar us forever; we seek stimulation and strive to stand out. If we're artistic, we hope for fame; if we're materialistic, we aim for riches; if we're spiritual, we hunger for enlightenment.

It's natural to seek out experience but it helps to realize that no single experience—not triumphs, not traumas—has a monopoly on defining your self-identity. Self-identity gets confused with appearance, and our appearances are thin as ice. It is easy to break through. On a crisp, cold day the stillness of a frozen lake is punctuated by a loud crack! This may kill us, or arouse us to life.

If we are attached to always running around and stirring things up, we do not give ourselves an opportunity to settle down to simplicity. If you have a glass of muddy water and try to clarify it by thrusting your fingers into it to pull out the little pieces of dirt, you will have a great deal of difficulty; the more you try, the more you'll disturb the muck. Let it sit still, though, and gradually the heavy sinks and settles.

In stillness water self-regulates and settles itself on itself. In doing so it becomes transparent. At that point, you can look through the vessel and see that glass and water together serve as a magnifying glass for your eye. The water glass functions as a lens, but when even the eye is forgotten, the glass is free and useless and renews itself in each gleam of light.

———

My qigong teacher, Master Liu, deeply venerates Buddhist practice but sometimes teases me: "Oh, you Buddhists, always concerned with suffering, illness, old age, and death! Always striving to become enlightened. We Taoists say, 'Just be natural! Live a long life! Be happy!'"

Perhaps this is not so different from what my Zen teacher, Sojun Mel Weitsman, means when he quotes his teacher (Shunryu Suzuki) as saying: "Don't be in such a hurry to get enlightened—you may not like it."

Enlightenment is nothing special; ordinary mind is the Way. We meditate not to become enlightened but to express how each of us already was, is, and will be enlightened together with every sentient being, every clod of mud, every bird and brick and tree.

There is no more and no less in enlightenment. You and I are each as enlightened as each other, as enlightened as our ancestors and our issue, profoundly ordinary and simple as uncarved wood.

We need to acknowledge our enlightened being. Bragging about spiritual awakening reveals its shallowness, but denying our experiences of realization turns our back on our true selves. How can we hope to live according to the Way if we see it as something far from us? How can we live fully to the best of our ability if we insist we lack enlightenment? Must we hold back until we've attained some extraordinary advanced state of being? I would suggest: Don't wait! Enlightenment is not separate from our ordinary muddles of being ourselves, so there is no need to stir things up by striving for purification.

One time I was describing an experience of insight during meditation to my sister and she asked me whether, "post-enlightenment," I still got depressed. I replied of course I do. Enlightenment does not add anything nor does it take anything away. But when depression tries to convince me despair is permanently etched into my soul, continuous practice makes it easier for me to remind myself of the truth of transience. Knowing no thing is permanent helps me keep faith in the possibility of renewal. Knowing the ice is slippery reminds me to watch my step.

16

Reach the pole of emptiness.
Abide, still, at the center.
Countless things coarising;
see them turn and re-turn.
Return to their roots, at their roots to be still.
In stillness recover, revive, and endure.
Always intimate with this: this is being illuminated.
Not mere illustration: not folly, but light.
All-embracing impartial: so kingly,
a firm haven like heaven, the firmament Way.
It underlies all;
past short or long longings,
beyond suffering: safe!

EVERYTHING IN THE WORLD is in motion. The arising and falling can make you dizzy: cars whizz past, people mill around, stock market bubbles pop, and sinkholes open up to swallow houses.

Look through a microscope and see the efflorescence of bacteria; look through a telescope and see the glowing edge of a black hole swallowing all that matters at its event horizon. Climb the stairs in your local hospital and you'll pass hospice on one level and the newborns' nursery on another.

It can feel as if you exist at the center of cacophonous commotion, like being in a boat where the scenery around you seems to be flowing past, when in fact the boat is moving too. We laugh at people who thought the earth was the center of the universe, but we are all egocentric, feeling our sense of ourselves—I am me—is the one constant in a changing world.

You are in the world, though, so everything in you is in motion too. As you read this, blood surges through your arteries and veins; in each cell of your body, molecules are moving. Messenger RNA wiggles out from the nucleus, travels past the ancient mitochondria of your ancestors, and traverses the cytoplasm of your self until it encounters the semipermeable membrane we call the cell wall. The bits and pieces of your being talk to each other within the cells of your senses, thoughts, feelings, impulses, and consciousnesses; they cross the semipermeable boundaries of the illusion of your self.

When you turn somersaults it looks like the world is turning topsy-turvy, but it is your body pivoting around the invisible center of the circle you make. When your emotions and thoughts churn, it seems like everything within is tumbling and crumbling, but it is your mind pivoting around the invisible center of the circle your self makes. This center cannot be seen, heard, touched, smelled, or tasted by your senses, but that doesn't mean it isn't there: you abide at the empty pivot point of yourself, still in the very midst of coming and going.

It may seem like your body is full of sensations and your mind is full of thoughts and feelings, each full of itself, each clamoring to claim your being as its own. Because the firmament of your self is empty, though, none of these ephemera can hold you for long: your self is always running freely, barefoot through the grasses of the world.

Beyond all the cell divisions, beyond the scrambling of molecules, beyond eating and drinking and sleeping and working, beyond pain and pleasure and beyond even living and dying, at your heart's center there is an indefinable crux that, however you express yourself and are expressed by others, can never be confined, harmed, or stained. In the midst of your busy life there is no need to suffer if you can be intimate with this stillness, with simply being yourself.

Turning and returning to this pivot point is not churning and rechurning, but tranquility in the midst of activity. The empty center of your self is impartial: it graces you with equanimity by treating all alike, allowing you to turn in any direction. You free yourself from desire not by ridding yourself of passion but by not clinging to any particular desire. Then you are safe: in boundless acceptance, however you tumble about, you are always coming home.

As a young boy I was anxious and restless. My parents used to say, using an old Yiddish phrase, that I sat as if I had "spielkes in tukhes"— splinters in my buttocks. Such a constitution is perhaps not the easiest preparation for sitting meditation calmly.

I struggled for years to abide still in my center during meditation. I would command myself: "Don't move!" and the sweat would pour down my forehead and my legs would tremble. My mind still wandered and my body ached.

I had no teacher at the time and drifted somewhat lost until my wandering took me to the top of Mount Diablo, an isolated peak rising 3,864 feet inland from the San Francisco Bay. At the summit I encountered a fist-sized salmon-colored sedimentary rock. The chert was pitted and jagged, but it called to me; without thinking much about it I picked it up and brought it home. For the next year my meditation consisted of simply sitting quietly, allowing my gaze to rest on the rock.

That rock kindly befriended me. It gave me some hint of how everything expresses itself by sitting in suchness. During my moves over the next few decades I mislaid my rough companion, but it is still with me. In fact wherever I am, here it is, and wherever it goes, there I am.

17

The best governor of your self, your world—
you barely know she exists.
The next best, you love and praise.
The next you respect out of fear.
And the last you despise and revile.
Not trusting in trust, mistrust arises.
Don't talk much about it;
just work quietly at it.
When the work has its fruit, allow people to say,
"It just happened naturally."

How MANY TIMES, as an adult, have you told yourself to "keep it together" in a world in which things are always falling apart? How many times, as a child, did you hear your parents say, "control yourself"?

Controlling yourself usually involves a bodily component, using muscle tension as a way of holding things in. Whether holding your bladder during a long car trip, biting your tongue when mad at a sibling, or blinking back your tears at a disappointment, we often interpret "control" as suppression. Fortunately, we can learn how to govern ourselves more easily, using modulation instead of suppression, by learning to trust in how life is self-organizing.

As a child you didn't need to give yourself instructions on how to grow an inch; as an adult you don't need to tell your heart to beat. You don't even need to tell yourself how to get up in the morning: have you ever found yourself waking a few minutes before your alarm clock was set to ring?

You don't need to tell yourself how to wake up, but you may need to remind yourself to go to bed on time. We become so active we forget to rest. If we alienate ourselves from the natural rhythms of our body by programming our life too much, we may override our internal regulators to the point where we can't fall asleep. Then the more we order ourselves to relax and drift off, the less we're able to do so.

There are physiological reasons for this. Ordering yourself engages the activating effects of the voluntary (sympathetic) nervous system, which blocks the vegetative regulatory effects of the involuntary (parasympathetic) nervous system. Artificial stimulants such as caffeine and electric light interfere with circadian rhythms. The fundamental problem, though, is that we lose trust in ourselves.

When we don't trust in our natural ability to fall asleep, we worry: when we worry, we can't sleep. The same holds true for most of our activities; the less we trust ourselves to get the job done, the more we over-think and interfere with the flow of the action.

We lose trust because there have been times in the past when we have not lived up to the expectations of ourselves and those around us, or others have not come through for us when we felt in need. Failure is not itself a problem—everybody fails, everybody makes mistakes—the problem comes when failure is contaminated by condemnation and loathing. We fear losing the respect and love of others, we fear our own helplessness and can despise ourselves for being "weak" or incompetent. Even if others love us and praise us for our accomplishments, we might feel that our successes are due to effortful effort and be insecure about what happens if we were to "just let go."

The fact is, you naturally self-regulate. If you provide your body with a modicum of regularity, it will relax into a rhythmic pattern and provide a healthy foundation allowing you to respond to novel demands. The same is true of the mind: let it settle, and it can organize, retrieve, and respond to experience. Have you ever had a word on the tip of your tongue, tried to command its appearance, finally given up, and then had it pop into your head minutes or hours later?

We go through many states of mind and states of being during a day. Governing yourself is not a matter of giving yourself orders, but of steering the ship of states. The boat is always moving; its natural buoyancy allows it to ride out storms and run with the wind, and only a small movement on the rudder or a slight adjustment of the sails is needed to adjust its course.

We may shrink a bit in the face of the vastness of the sea, but we can rely on water being wet, on the ocean's ability to hold up whatever floats, and on wind pervading everywhere. When you take good care of the vessel that bears you, it's natural for her to return the favor and compassionately uphold you on seas stormy or calm, whether you are muddling though dense fogs or skipping along under clear skies.

———

Recently I spent two months by myself in the canyonlands of Utah. I intended to get up every morning at 5 a.m., meditate, then hike with a light backpack to my next campsite. I was unhappy when I (frequently) slept more than I intended. I became frustrated with myself for not getting up sooner and not taking full advantage of my time in the wilderness.

One morning I woke up quite a bit later than planned and was annoyed with myself. Then I noticed something was missing: I didn't hear any bird song. It was still dark. And cold. I realized the sun had not reached the deep declivity of the canyon, so the birds, not being stupid, were not up before the warmth and light of the sun.

I thought it might be wise to take a cue from the birds and stop fighting with myself about being "lazy." Since I had entered the wilderness, my body had been wanting to go to sleep when it got dark and wake up when it got light.

The rest of my trip I followed the schedule of sun and moon. My meditation became more natural and less forced; I felt I was drawing on sources of sustenance beyond myself and enjoyed more energy than I'd known for many years.

18

When the Way is forgotten,
benevolence and righteousness arise.
When knowledge and reason rule,
so does artificiality and deceit.
When family relationships are not harmonious,
then there is "dutifulness" and "love."
When a country is in dark disorder,
then officials proclaim themselves "virtuous."

WE CAN MISTAKE self-awareness for mindfulness. Self-awareness, though, can easily become self-centeredness, at which point any quality we assign to ourselves can become an anchor for a self-image.

When we become attached to a self-image we become invested in maintaining it. If I perform some act of kindness, there is a tendency to start thinking of myself as a kindly person. If I practice forbearance in the face of someone's anger and act sweetly reasonable, I may congratulate myself for not returning anger with anger and then feel self-righteous. If we perceive a threat to our carefully constructed kindly persona, though, our image can break down in an aggressive explosion.

It's easy to fall into the trap. We're all a bit like Groucho Marx in the movie *Duck Soup*: Groucho decides to go over to his enemy's house and offer him the hand of friendship. On the way there he tells himself what a wonderful fellow he is to be so forgiving. But then he thinks, "But suppose I offer him the hand of friendship, and he doesn't take my hand? Where will I be then? What a humiliation that will be! How dare he turn down the hand of friendship! That's an insult!" By the time he arrives at his destination he's so worked up that as soon as his enemy's door opens Groucho yells "Insult *me*, will you!" slaps the face of the (silent, bemused) person who answers the door, and shouts, "This means war!"

We separate ourselves from ourselves when we cling too tightly to our positive persona. Then self-consciousness can make what is natural into something forced and artificial. When families stayed close together, there was no call for Mother's Day cards and demonstrations of love: you lived the truth of intimacy, with its fluctuations of selfishness and selflessness, gratitude and frustration, cooperating together and working apart. It was only after families were separated by distance, jobs, or politics that Mother's Days became necessary, but taking Mom out to dinner as an artificial social obligation instead of as a naturally arising impulse is an exercise in family politics, not an expression of love.

Politicians often trumpet moral values; they try to attract votes by proclaiming themselves virtuous. All of us are subject to the same temptation because we're all engaged in the politics of competing interests. Interests compete when they are based on self-interest; self-interest arises from attachment to desires; desire arises in the service of feeding a personal identity. When conflicts arise, we may try to trump our opponent's position by insisting our values (which we see as central to our identity) have greater moral virtue. This is intellectual virtuosity in the service of power, not governance.

When we become attached to our self-centered moral values they become mere ways of looking good to others instead of guidelines for finding our Way. When we see there is no "me" without "you," we seek a path that emerges bigger than either one of us, and good government arises from the attempt to form a more perfect union.

I found myself getting annoyed with my travel companion on a two-month trek. He could seem over-sure of himself, critical and belittling—too close to my own faults to be comfortable. My attempts to talk with him about what was happening between us didn't go anywhere so I resolved to take responsibility for my cranky ego and transform irritation to "benevolence." I started chanting a mantra to myself as I hiked, repeating it over and over again, using my steps to establish a rhythm. I preceded each repetition with the intention "transform ego into blessings for the land, my companions, and all beings." However, I soon became aware of how subtle my ego can be. A thought arose: "I could help him if he'd let me." Very sincere, very virtuous, and very much putting me in a one-up position.

I struggled to divest myself of some of this self-centeredness. I started counting backward with each mantra from 108 to zero, and with each decreasing number consciously tried to let go of any egoistic concerns. Sometimes I'd have a brief stretch of egolessness, but very quickly the egoistic thought "Hey! I managed to be free of ego for a bit" would pop up. Then more thoughts and feelings followed.

I had to smile. Wishing to be rid of ego was itself an egoistic, self-centered mode of being. I relaxed and, instead of artificially trying to purify myself with forced benevolence, I began to welcome each shred of ego as fuel for composting. Then the heat of the decaying compost generated energy for the hike. I was more able to enjoy the pleasure of just walking, the tread of the trail underfoot, finding my way in its ups and downs.

19

Eliminate knowledge, discard reason—
people live a hundred times better.
Eliminate benevolence, discard righteousness—
families flourish in compassion.
Eliminate craftiness, discard profit—
no more robbers or thieves.
The three above are not quite enough,
so a little advice:
be plain as undyed silk,
genuine as uncarved wood,
reduce self-importance,
limit desires.
No need for more learning;
no undue concern.

YOU CAN REASON with your ego, but it won't necessarily listen. You can't reason your way to selflessness.

Virtuously suppressing the feeling of being virtuous doesn't work. If you rely only on reason and knowledge to govern yourself you turn the mind into an instrument of rationalization instead of a vehicle for realization.

You cannot find your way through life in a purely rational fashion, because reason can justify pretty much any stance you choose to adopt.

As Benjamin Franklin once remarked, it is very convenient to be a reasonable creature, because "it enables one to find or make a reason for everything one has a mind to do."

On the other hand, if you reject reason's role in guiding your life and give yourself up purely to the play of emotions, you risk being ruled by hungry desires that will eat you up. Although we are inherently without self, we are still self-centered. However "enlightened" we may be, nobody is beyond gain and loss and the unconscious desires that often drive our actions.

We share with all living beings an innate tendency to repeat what we find pleasurable and shrink from what gives us pain. It is easy to become confused if these are the only forces you listen to, and if you think moral values are only subjective preferences you can arrive at a place where everything is "okay" but then discover that nothing is okay. If you use cultural relativism to righteously denounce self-righteousness, then why not live a life of untrammeled hedonism? Without clear standards, how do you condemn torture and genocide?

The middle way between reason and feeling, benevolence and detachment, craftiness and innocence, is not a halfway point. Freeing ourselves from intellectualization does not mean situating ourselves at some compromise between cold thought and hot emotion, just as freeing ourselves from the fetters of self-aggrandizement does not mean finding our place halfway to humiliation.

The middle way is the central way. It is not halfway on a line between two extremes but resides in an entirely different dimension: it is just natural. When you can acknowledge knowledge but are not limited by it, when you can think beyond thinking, feel beyond feeling, and center on your original unconditioned self, compassion arises.

In the Holocaust Museum in Washington, D.C., there is an exhibit showing people who, at risk to their own welfare, protected Jews by hiding them from the Nazis. One German couple, uneducated farmers, were asked why they had secretly harbored a Jewish family throughout the war. As I remember their response, it was: "To tell you the truth,

we've never liked Jews. But it doesn't matter; killing and torturing people is just plain wrong."

I felt deeply moved by their words. When like these people we can
go beyond our personal preferences, opinions, and ideology, the Way
appears as plain and simple truth: genocide is unnatural, compassion
unforcedly flows. If a child is about to run out into the street, you rush
to stop him without thinking. If you have plenty of food and the person
next to you is hungry, you spontaneously offer some of what you have.

These unpremeditated impulses are genuine since they are independent of your personal preferences, beyond what you want to do or even
what you feel you ought to do. The middle way is just the path that
meets the needs of the moment in the most natural fashion.

Being natural is simple but not always easy. Most of us find it is
difficult to trust ourselves. We have been so conditioned to protect
ourselves from both the cruelty of others and our own base instincts
we sometimes mistrust even kindness, and we erect guards against our
innocence.

It is your innocent unguarded self, though, that shares a natural
impulse with the dog who licks your face when you are lonely and
the tree whose leafy branches unthinkingly shield you from the storm.
Compassion need not be "reasonable," but it is always wise.

Your heartwood is supple and pure. All you need do is be natural.
Open up and let be: desires come and go, thought-bubbles form and
pop, impulses wax and wane. There is freedom to be found.

—

When I was teaching on a Fulbright in India I would often take my
two young daughters to a small park. While there, sometimes other
children came up to me and, though we were strangers to each other,
they'd say, "Uncle, can I have a drink of water?" I would take them to
the water fountain, hold them up to get some sips, and then they would
go back to wherever they had been playing. Neither the child nor I

thought much about it. A child was thirsty: I would help him or her drink water. Very simple.

Currently in the United States we seem to have lost trust in such natural acts and teach our children to beware of strangers. But it wasn't always this way.

One of my strongest childhood memories is of being at the beach when I was around four years old. I loved to roll in the sand. I would roll away from my family's blanket then roll back: roll further away, then roll back again. One day, though, I rolled far enough away that when I sat up I saw a sea of beach umbrellas, and sand and water, but no Mommy or Daddy.

I started to cry. Some strangers noticed me and, realizing I was lost, they took me to a little enclosure where there were other lost children. I remember they bought me an ice cream. The enclosure had a fence and some grasses and trees, with a rabbit darting through the undergrowth. I, together with all the children, delighted in looking for, losing, then finding the rabbit. My distressed parents came to retrieve me, expecting to find a very scared child, but I didn't want to stop chasing the bunny.

I don't recall the faces of the strangers who helped me. But I have a visual memory of their hands, and a tactile sense of their warmth as they took my hand in theirs.

20

Yes, no: not far apart.

Beautiful, ugly; good, evil: not unalike.

Fear the mind-killer spreads contagion to all,

but I am the wilderness, still before dawn.

Everyone else parties wild and frenetic,

while I sit here silent, a child prior to form,

a newborn who hasn't yet learned how to smile,

lost in the nebula, homeless alone.

While the many have much,

I the fool stay so simple.

All the people are certain they see things quite clearly;

I still wander in darkness,

with the waves in the waters,

with the winds playing ceaseless on oceans so deep.

Everyone has a goal.

I am useless and stupid,

lowly and lacking.

I now go on alone,

but I meet myself everywhere,

supping on, sipping, always sustained,

by our mother's Great Source.

You ARE NEVER far apart from yourself, even when you feel sundered by contradictory impulses.

We all want to be special and stand out, but we also want to be just like everybody else and blend in. We all want our life to be uncomplicated, predictable, and simple, but we also want it to be exciting, surprising, and complex. We fear we cannot contain our contradictions, that we'll be flung into bits and pieces by the centrifugal forces pulling us in what logic tells us are mutually exclusive directions. Fortunately, your natural being is large beyond logic.

Like all living beings we take in and excrete, go forward and back, live and die. Like all animals, we sleep and wake up; like all mammals (and all birds, in fact) we dream. Seen against the background of these fundamentals, the distinctions that divide us—what we humans call fame and fortune, being popular or unfashionable, loved, hated, or ignored—shrink in importance. They are not the kinds of differences that truly make a significant difference; perhaps these markings are just the stuff of dreams, and we the stuff that dreams are made on.

Most of us live in the world of dreams, where what clothes you wear may determine what job you hold and what friends will (or will not) congregate around you. We clothe ourselves in our personas. We so easily define ourselves: married (or single), pretty (or homely), a prisoner, a stock-trader, a battle-tested soldier. It feels the role we are playing determines who we are, and we hope the door of our dressing room will be distinguished by a star.

You don't need accolades to confirm you. You emerge from the womb with a unique set of genes and identifiable fingerprints; soon you will have your own way of nursing and spitting out, rolling over and sitting up. You learn how to walk with your own unique gait, and as you bump into the world your phenotype shapes into its various forms. Soon you'll be socialized to separate work from play, competition from cooperation, self from other; lost in the glare of artificial illumination, your desires lead you to develop skills and plan for profits. Pursuing your goals, convincing others you are useful and worthy, you may lose sight of how being, itself, is enough.

Go off to solitude, though, far from cities and towns, and the night skies will be darker and the constellations more bright. A single candle flame can be seen from miles away. There, as Mary Oliver says, "whoever you are, no matter how lonely, the world offers itself to you." At the same moment you are a lens of the world by which it sees itself.

When you come across a stream you realize you are just another form of water, but this water quenches your thirst; when you eat a piece of fruit you become a vehicle of its seed, but it is the burning of its sugars that provides the energy for your actions; when you stumble on a tuft of grass you realize you too are a form of earth, but the ground supports you where you stand and catches you when you fall. You don't need a goal for the Great Mother to sustain you and bring you to your natural fruition.

———

Things ripen of their own accord.

One day I was on the way to my teacher Sojun Weitsman and saw a small plum tree where the fruit was hanging heavy but still green. I said to my teacher that I felt like the plum: I was ripening but not there yet.

Sojun replied: "The difference between you and the plum . . . is that the plum doesn't worry about it."

21

True virtue is empty;
it flows from the Way.
The Way waxes and wanes like the breath, in and out.
No form and no shape but an image arises,
ungraspable, coursing but darkly substantive,
evasive, intangible: seeding the fundament.
Heart of the Real, the genuine life,
eternal, unchanged,
our ancestors' call
never ceasing,
its origin known through its nature,
just this.

I am not virtuous. It is too much work. Vice and iniquity, though, require even more work.

In these days of political correctness and cultural relativity, it's fashionable to assert there is no such thing as truth. This assertion is false. Truth exists: it's just that it is not fixed in place. Truth is alive and so it grows and shrinks, transforms into unexpected shapes as it is refracted through more minds, more people, more experience.

There's no particular merit to telling the truth, but keeping track of what lies you've told gets more and more difficult since the truth is always threatening to poke its inconvenient nose out. I find it's easier, on the whole, to tell the truth.

In any case, I've always been a very poor liar. On the rare occasions where I succeeded initially in convincing someone that my lie was actually the truth, it was hard subsequently to remember enough of the details to keep track of what I had and had not said. Finding that lying made me anxious and uneasy, I stopped.

When you stop using lies for the easy excuse, knowing what to omit and how to phrase what you say takes a bit of tact and a modicum of the art of editing. Ultimately, though, it is easier to be genuine than to be artificial; cosmetics will wear off in tears and kisses, smear in downpours, and fade in harsh sunlight. Our skin is absorbent and our environment abrasive: between the two, any veneer is bound to fail.

It is easier to be who you are than to try to stick to some prewritten role you have imagined for yourself: life has a way of not following the script. Who you are can include—but is bigger than—your imaginings. If you think you have to know who you are to be yourself you will become frustrated. Who you are is ungraspable: your "who" is an every-changing being.

Fortunately, you don't need to know who you are to be who you are. Being body, minding the moment, you hear the call of your true self and commune with the source of your life. You know when you ring true, and so does everybody else.

When you refrain from unwholesome actions, are not caught by holding on or by pushing away, when you are compassionate to everyone, not caught by your fantasies or deceived by your thoughts, not anticipating the future or summoning the past, you will be intimate with your life as it is right now. This is you.

———

I used to get very anxious when people got mad at me. I would try to push away my nervousness, but in my anxiety my mouth would start shaping itself into a sickening grin.

I felt this grin came across as both demeaning and challenging; I feared the other person would feel insulted by it and escalate their anger. So I'd suppress the grin and try to maintain an appearance of calm. In doing so my anxiety would increase and the muscles around my lips start to tighten even more. I would wrestle in an uncomfortable fight with myself while I was simultaneously trying to respond to the other's exasperation. I spent a good deal of time trying, and to some extent succeeding, in understanding the sources of my anxiety. Unfortunately, neither insight nor relaxation exercises did much to alleviate the pattern.

After some years of struggling with this, I finally decided that pretending wasn't working. I resolved the next time someone got mad at me, if I felt the push of a nervous grin I'd allow it to happen, and if the other person reacted, I'd simply explain: I wasn't trying to be disrespectful, I was anxious and the grin was an expression of my nervousness.

To my surprise, as soon as I felt comfortable being more transparent, the urge to grin vanished. Robbed of the ally of suppression, my anxiety diminished as well.

Within a few months of my becoming more truthful with myself and others about my anxiety, my work as a psychologist found me locked in a cell with a violent and very angry prisoner who threatened to "wipe the floor" with me. We were alone in an isolated cell block; there was no panic button and the nearest guards were some distance away. My ability to be genuine in responding to this man's anger probably helped preserve my life.

22

Supple bending, the whole unbroken;
crookedly wandering the path, you'll go straight;
hollowing yourself leaves you room to feel full;
worn out, renewal.
With less you're contented, with more you're confused.
Embracing the One as a guide for the world,
not watching yourself, you appear yourself fully.
Don't go out and shine; don't go in and hide.
No excuses, no brags: your merit untarnished.
Unhindered by pride, your model endures.
Not contending with others, there's no competition.
The old saying is "supple bending, unbroken";
bowing deeply, sincerely,
you're completed and whole.

"NEVER GIVE IN! Never surrender!" firms up our boundaries and sharpens our sense of what we stand for. This kind of inspiration, though, often suffers a premature expiration; "heroic" recalcitrance invites exhaustion and confrontations that may end in violence or even death.

We often think being faithful to ourselves means not giving in to circumstances or compromising. Politicians sign clear pledges that bolster their standings but perilously ignore messy realities. Zen meditators sit through pain that sometimes leads to breakthroughs of insight but other times leads to broken knees.

When we adopt rigid positions we define ourselves not by what we stand for but what we are against. "You can't do that to me" puffs us up but is close cousin to a two-year-old's assertion of self through the power of "No!" This is no power at all, but mere temper; when you find your position through opposition, you narrow your options. Such stances are not integral to you but merely a borrowed reflection of your adversary.

Many of my generation learned to define themselves in opposition to the war in Vietnam. When the war ended, many drifted. Today it seems people on the right define themselves by objecting to the morality of those on the left, people on the left define themselves by objecting to being controlled by others' notions of morality, and people in the center define themselves by objecting to the objectors. Such definitions are not sustainable: they are serious crimps in a rigid body politic where people no longer listen to each other but only to those who already agree with them.

Your true self is not a stone statue to a cause but a dancer finding herself in the playful surprise of moving moments. You are not a thing but a constantly evolving ecology of body and mind with flexible boundaries, just as the line that divides forest from meadow is a flux, not a fence.

Sailors on the living sea know they cannot go from point A to point B in a straight line but have to tack back and forth to take account of shifting winds. This does not condone deceit or hypocrisy, nor imply that all means can be justified by their ends. It merely warns us not to be pinned down by our opinions, not to worry so much about saving face that we set our features in a mask. Walking in the mountains, sticking to a narrow path can dig deep ruts in fragile meadows, but this doesn't mean you must trample the most delicate flowers to find an alternate route. If you meet someone coming the opposite way on a narrow trail, there are many options other than pushing for prominence or shrinking from the encounter.

Being yourself is not a contest. I cannot become more "me" by defeating "you," and if I am defeated by you in a competition I can lose the game without losing my self. You and I might vie over a job, an election, a sports championship, or a lover; our desires may be at stake in the outcome, but not our sense of who we are.

Don't mistake your desires for who you are. Winning may give you more problems than losing, which may give you opportunities you'd never seen before.

Beyond winning and losing, why not cooperate? Bowing to a friend does not diminish self-respect, it strengthens the respect we hold for our friendship. At the start of a contest, if we bow to our opponent and honor our meeting, the result—win or loss—will be a mutual honing of skill and a furthering of our craft.

———

I was teaching a qigong class with a good friend assisting me. After I completed introducing a particular move my friend started describing it differently. I was annoyed: she was not following my class plan and was taking up time without consulting me beforehand. I was especially irritated because her instructions were in many ways better than mine.

My pride was hurt: wasn't I supposed to be the lead teacher? I was ashamed of myself for feeling competitive, but I found myself silently finding fault with small details of what she was doing.

At the end of the class I verbally guide my students through all sixty-four movements of the form while doing the movements with them. This takes some effort. Peevishly, I asked my friend to take on the task so I could stand back, watch, and critique what she was doing. She willingly took her place at the front but surprised me by requesting that instead of watching, I do the form at the back so students would have a model to observe when they turned around. I stifled my annoyance at her contravening my wishes and took my place.

As she guided us through the form I started to relax and let go of how rigid I had been. I was able to see how our students, given the opportunity, learned from each of us and from each other. As we flowed through the qigong together a palpable sense of peace and wholeness arose in the room. I found some new insights into the movements and felt grateful to my friend.

When we completed the form, we bowed to each other, and I thanked her for her teaching.

23

Nature does not make long speeches.
Fierce winds blow themselves out in one morning.
Thunderstorms' torrents give way to clear skies.
Heaven-and-Earth is their author but they don't last long:
mustn't human creation taste impermanence too?
As you practice the Way, you are shaped by the Way;
as you practice integrity you are shaped by true nature;
as you practice with failure you are shaped by loss.
Practice finds you and the Way mutually welcoming;
by virtue of being, Rightness meets you with joy.
Letting go you are welcomed at peace in your loss.
Sincerity, trust:
without them, faith fails.

PASSIONS PASS, but we habitually hold on to our desires even after the tempests have subsided.

This can be particularly true of sexual desires. Our lusty gusts blow themselves out, but these transient storms can leave their mark on us and those around us. If we treat our sexuality as an emblem of our identity rather than a climatic condition, we can confuse sex and love; this can lead to suppression or indulgence, pleading or blaming both ourselves and our lovers as we hurtle between longing and loathing.

Sexuality is natural, but precisely because it is natural it is marked with impermanence. Trysts can be tricky and satiation is not a solution to hunger, since it can never be anything other than temporary.

This doesn't mean you should not act on sexual arousal or, for that matter, any other emotional squall. Whether you brave the weather of intimacy depends not only on rain or shine but also on the level of your supplies at home, the urgency of the tasks awaiting you outside, and the clothing you have available to wear. If you go out in a downpour you're likely to get wet even wearing the best Gore-Tex jacket, and if you stay out in a harsh sun at a high altitude, the thin air ensures you'll get burned even wearing sunblock. On the other hand, if you don't go out, your supplies may dwindle, your skin will turn ashen, and the vacuity of missed opportunities will drain you of vitality.

No matter what you do—stay back or go ahead—all your actions have consequences for yourself and others. These consequences are both far-reaching and short-lived. They are short-lived because something else will quickly follow. They are far-reaching because they form a link in an endless chain. This is particularly true when we are at our most vulnerable: when our love is intermixed with need.

At such times it may feel if you reveal yourself fully you'll open yourself to hurts you cannot bear, but if you hide yourself you'll never receive the embrace you need. Acceptance and rejection are strong tides in our lives, and their ebb and rise influences the flow of sex and love.

Love depends on whether we are able to face hurt, impermanence, and loss with deep sincerity. Trust does not grow in the easy reassurance of shallow, casual encounters. Trust grows when we acknowledge the depth of our needs, the pains of our losses, and the inevitability of our disappointments yet still extend faith to our lover and ourselves, practicing full engagement and mutual welcoming. Ultimately, there is no way forward into intimacy except through integrity.

You don't need an encyclopedic knowledge of yourself, complete with index and table of contents, to sense whether or not you are acting with integrity. Just be honest with yourself. Being yourself means acknowledging everything you do, accepting the consequences of your actions without casting blame for sin or protesting your innocence.

When you meet someone wholeheartedly their responses tell you not only something about who they are but about who you are. You meet yourself meeting your lover by recognizing that his or her moods and needs are as changeable as your own.

———

Depression has been a frequent visitor to my house. Depression has a central lie: it insists (and feels) it is forever. Years of practice (Zen, qigong, psychotherapy) have softened depression's edges by illuminating the truth of impermanence. Still, I sometimes get depressed. Then I feel tired and want to withdraw. At such times I dislike telling others I'm depressed; I (falsely) feel it indicates some failure as a therapist, as a teacher and practitioner of Zen and qigong.

After one morning's meditation and qigong I mentioned to my partner I was struggling with depression. We didn't discuss it as we each rushed off to the day's activities, but later that day I got a phone call from her. I didn't want to answer the call. I preferred to swathe myself in a cocoon, to avoid discussing the logistics of our weekend plans. But I am in a relationship, so I picked up the phone.

She wasn't calling about logistics. She called to say she'd heard me say I was struggling and just wanted to let me know she was available if I needed her. If I wanted space to myself, she would offer it; if I wanted to drop by her place, she would feed me "something yummy."

Not surprisingly, my mood improved.

24

A person on tiptoes cannot stand steady.

A person who straddles cannot walk far.

A person who sees only himself sees very little.

A person who offers justifications will not be admired.

A show-off will fail to be a good leader.

Praise yourself and you really will not achieve much.

Those who travel the Way say,

"Too much food, excess action: superfluous, bad."

Avoid such indulgence, be one with the Way.

IF FEAR KEEPS YOU from committing yourself and you straddle decisions, you are neither here nor there. On a hot day at the beach if
you just dabble a toe in the cold water, your footing is precarious; the
undertow may sweep you away.

When you are divided within yourself, worrying about making the
right decision, you fret whether your choice will take you on a path that
leads to what you want. You may be less aware of another source of uneas-
iness: how your choice will affect your image of yourself. Failure may put
dings in your self-esteem while success may raise expectations that create
more pressure.

We like to make a big splash. What fun to stomp our feet as we rush
in to the water, so that everyone knows we're coming! How tempting it
is to stand at home plate and admire the home run you've just hit—even

though you know this may motivate the pitcher to throw at you the next time you come up to the plate. Display your diplomas and people will hang on your every word, trumpet your trophies and you will be besieged with endorsements, be a singing idol and you can grope your groupies to your heart's content.

Or not. Being on the cover of *People* is a pretty good predictor of misery to come. People will gossip about the images they project onto you; your audience may admire your fame but will be titillated by your shortcomings. It becomes harder to concentrate on your craft when your energy is occupied by celebrations of yourself and the need to protect your idealized image.

Any ambivalence you have about committing yourself to a choice is magnified when you see those choices solely from the standpoint of how they affect *you*. If you choose a career solely on the basis of whether you will enjoy the work and how well it pays, you may find yourself employing your skills in the service of causes you once would have found repugnant. If you choose a husband or wife solely on the basis of whether that person pleases you, you may find yourself getting divorced later on because you fail to please him or her.

Vision limited to yourself is not only short-sighted but short-term: it does not take into account the way the ripples you create come back to you. Some call this *karma*, but you do not need a fancy word to recognize that every action you take has consequences that go beyond yourself. In traditional societies, it is taken for granted that the choices a young person makes affect not just himself but also his family and community. In our individualistic society we tend to overlook this; instead we are told that we can be anything we want to be, as if the most important thing is to indulge our personal wants.

Group cohesion and individual satisfaction are related, not opposed; you and your world constitute an ecology of independence and interdependence intertwined. You leave traces of yourself everywhere you go, as the world engraves itself on and in you. The more you make choices that complement or harmonize with your greater surroundings, the more likely it is you won't have to face unintended negative consequences.

People remember the first words of Whitman's "I celebrate myself and sing myself," but forget the lines that follow:

> And what I assume you shall assume,
> For every atom belonging to me,
> As good as belongs to you.

The world does not belong to you: we belong to each other.

———

I was twenty-six when I got married. I felt ambivalent about fully committing myself to the relationship, and although I loved my wife I wondered whether I had settled down too soon.

My wife and I cared about each other deeply; we were good partners raising our children, and we enjoyed our travels and adventures together. I wrote my wife sonnets, supported her in her career choices, and tried to surprise her with gifts I hoped she'd like, but underneath our genuine happiness my ambivalence persisted. My wife sensed my inner hesitation and felt very hurt by it.

After some years I was able to let go of my doubts and devote myself wholeheartedly to our marriage, but I was too late; the wounds had left scars and in reaction to them (along with certain inner struggles of her own) my wife began to withdraw from me. When our children were grown, after thirty years of marriage, she left me.

We still care about each other and stay in touch. We've acknowledged the scars and blocks we each had which, despite our good intentions, in subtle ways reinforced each others' hesitations. Somehow those had lived in an unmetabolized region of our relationship so that, straddling intimacy issues for too long, we lost our balance.

Perhaps it was only through this painful path that I could learn to see beyond myself. My current partner and I try to be fully present to each other. Simple-though-not-always-easy honesty provides the ground on which we try to truly see both each other and our selves.

25

Prior to heaven, prior to earth,
existing spontaneous, formless, complete,
silent, ungraspable,
standing as suchness, not altering, lone,
traveling everywhere, cyclical movement,
everywhen reaching, never exhausted,
mother to everyone, heaven and earth:
not knowing its name, I call it the Way.
If forced to picture it,
I call it "vast."
Being vast, it is ever-flowing;
ever-flowing, it reaches far;
reaching far, it returns to itself.
Way being vast,
heaven is vast,
earth is vast,
the true sovereign also is vast.
In the realm, four vastnesses,
and the true sovereign is one of them.
Humans conform with earth,
earth conforms with heaven,
heaven conforms with the Way making itself.
The Way conforms to its nature:
spontaneous, such.

LOOKED AT ONE WAY, there is no creation and no destruction, just a constant reshuffling of matter and energy. Here we do not have birthdays and funerals: every day is (as Thich Nhat Hanh says) "continuation day." Like the moon, you seem to wax and wane, but these apparent phases are illusions cast by passing shadows: your true face is, was, and will ever be.

Looked at from a different perspective, universes are constantly coming into being and going into nonbeing. The singularity of spontaneous generation and the black hole from which nothing returns are always at work. You embody this. While you are reading these words new cells are coming into being within you, new dendrites and axons are spreading their fingers to neighboring neurons; some of your cells are devouring others, some are decaying and dying.

You are a unique expression of these two perspectives of the cosmos: you are complete in yourself, constantly changing yet never altering. Flowing to the outermost limits of your experience and returning to the ungraspable center of your being, you are a vehicle through which the universe actualizes itself. The vastness of our being fills us with an awe close kin to terror. Who's in charge? We cannot control our brain to think only wise thoughts nor teach our marrow how to build our bones: we cannot even will ourselves to sleep. In a panic you tell yourself to breathe and feel you cannot, yet if you collapse into the faint you fear, your breath will return of its own accord.

We rest on foundations vaster and wiser than our conscious will. We can be spontaneous because we can rely on what exists prior to its arising. It is a peculiarity of our nervous system that signals flash from brain to muscle before we are aware of the impulse to move; creative ideas arise before we know how to phrase them in words or shape them into forms of art.

You cannot micromanage the basis of your being, but you can guide its expression. You can shape and mold the clay of your life and even the spirit of your death. You cannot tell your heart to beat but you can influence its rhythm and its speed through exercise and diet; you cannot force your heart to love but you can summon compassion and kindness for all you encounter.

You touch, and are touched by, the world. You shape yourself by responding as best you can to what is immediately in front of you. As your unique self and your specific circumstances encounter each other in each place and each time, the situation turns and, in turning, discovers that what seemed to be boundaries in fact are horizons. Each of us exists beyond our knowledge, stretching limitlessly backward and forward in time.

Even before conception you were alive in the twinkle of your parents' eyes, in the love that led to your parents' union, and in the love of their parents' parents and all who preceded them. The same holds true for after as it does before. Even after your death the ripples of your existence permeate the lives of all you have interacted with; the elements of your being are taken up by your successors whether these be human children, earthworms, or plants rooted in the organic matter you leave behind. No matter how well we think we know people, we cannot know what they will be like tomorrow, let alone in ten centuries.

Every being that exists is always making herself anew and thus is infinite, vast. This is true for ourselves as well. When we seek the true sovereign of our self we find he always conforms to his nature: ungraspable and ever-flowing.

———

Parents often want their children to grow up to conform to the parents' expectations, but because children reach back beyond their birth and forward beyond their parents' deaths they are vast in their own being.

When my youngest daughter was preparing to be married she asked me to walk her down the aisle at her wedding. I said I thought I might be pretty emotional as I gave her away.

"Dad," she said, "It's not like I belong to you; you can't give me away."

May I always see my daughter as herself: ungraspable, spontaneous, such.

26

The heavy anchors the light;
equanimity masters restlessness.
The sage traveling all day stays close to his supplies
in protected encampments, calm amid noise,
undisturbed, finds his place.
Should a lord of ten thousand chariots
treat himself more lightly than he treats the whole world?
Too light: you lose your foundation.
Too restless: you lose your mastery.

WE OFTEN LET OUR minds run on and on without anchoring them in equanimity; we push our bodies without grounding them in repose. Thinking, feeling, responding to all we encounter—solving problems, speaking our mind, biting our tongue, driving in traffic—all of these take energy.

We are learning the resources of the earth are not inexhaustible and are beginning to practice conservation, but we often expend ourselves without any consideration of how our own resources can be depleted. If we're operating a car, we usually try to refill the gas tank before it gets all the way to empty; unfortunately we aren't as careful to check our body's energy gauge and monitor our mind's clarity. Our supplies of serenity are always close at hand, but we push ourselves and defer recharging our spirits and revitalizing our strength until "later"; we get so used to being in active mode we become addicted to stimulation and feel restless when we try to stop.

If you simply sit quietly, at a certain point you will journey past restlessness. Initially you may find yourself obsessing over what you have to do, or be flooded with feeling, or perhaps memories and fantasies will fill the space in your mind. Eventually, though, your mind will empty itself: you will either calm down, get bored, or fall asleep from exhaustion. This is a basic law of thermodynamics; high-energy, agitated states settle down naturally if left undisturbed.

Maintaining composure in the face of the noisy world is a skill that needs practice, so it helps to begin in protected environments. Create a quiet time and place to exercise stillness: set aside all involvement and let the myriad things rest. If the phone rings or the doorbell chimes during this time, don't answer it. Give your body and mind a chance to become familiar with relaxed calm; each time you cultivate this foundation makes it easier to return to it.

During daily life when you encounter hurdles, the first thing to do is to not do anything. Use the method you learned as a child to cross the street: stop, look, and listen. Don't try to solve things too soon, or your actions will just make the situation more unclear. Check in with your current internal state: is it resilient enough to deal with the obstacle? If not, first do what's necessary to nurture yourself with food, sleep, friendship, and your allies in nature.

Once you're ready to look at the difficulty, ask yourself: have you been up against it before? If so, what has helped? What hasn't helped, despite your repeated efforts? So many problems are maintained by our efforts to solve them: if your effort hasn't worked after giving it a good try, stop repeating an exercise in futility.

This takes patience. Patience, though, is not the forced frustration of waiting but the art of staying close to your supplies, of remaining in touch with the undisturbed center of your being. When you wait, you anticipate what comes next and want to hurry along, so you feel restless and on edge. Patience is more pleasant: settling into the situation at hand so you can take stock of what's around you and notice more.

Standing in line for a movie, instead of tapping your foot and checking your watch to see how many minutes remain before the show, relax: feel your feet on the ground, and observe the crowd around you. You'll probably find something interesting or entertaining if you look with curiosity. Sitting in highway traffic in your car, instead of fruitlessly peering out to see how all the other lanes seem to be moving faster, let gravity help you unwind. Use the slowdown to loosen the hands that are gripping the steering wheel so tightly; drop your elbows and relax the shoulders that have tensed up as high as your ears.

Patience requires acceptance, but acceptance doesn't mean resignation: it means seeing a situation clearly without adding or subtracting anything from it. This is easier said than done, since we color our situations with filters according to how we would like things to be. But acceptance builds a deeper foundation in reality: it's easier to master a situation if you are dealing with what is actually in front of you, which is usually larger than you are aware of.

When you journey in the ship of yourself, you may only notice the waves, the wind, and a shore that seems distant, but you are always supported by the ocean floor underneath and the air all around you. Patience creates a larger space in which you can breathe easy by anchoring yourself in the place where you are.

—

I've never been very fond of committee meetings. It took me too many years to realize that meetings' ostensible purpose (sifting information, making decisions and plans) is subordinate to their real one: letting people feel heard. This often means letting people go round and round a topic, repeating themselves without listening to each other. I recognize this, but I still sometimes get frustrated by the noise of egos clashing.

I've learned it helps to make a comfortable encampment for myself: I bring a cushion for my chair so I can sit straight but at ease. I place the tip of my tongue so it lightly touches my upper palate; this helps my facial muscles relax and also serves as a kind of early warning system (if I start to tense, my tongue begins to press too hard; if my mind wanders, my tongue starts moving around as well). I also often do a little acupressure self-massage, my favorite points being *laogong* (near the center of the palm) and *neiguan* (about two finger-widths up from the wrist, between the tendons of the inner lower arm). Both points are good for anxiety and tension.

It also helps to have a cup of green tea. There's something about a teacup that asks to be held gently, with two hands; the tea itself not only alerts but soothes. If a meeting gets too contentious, I'll serve tea to all the participants and the discussion usually calms down: it's hard to shout when you're sipping and hard to wave your hands around when they're holding a warm teacup.

I like to keep my tea supplies close by; they're allies of equanimity.

27

Good traveling leaves no trace,
good speaking leaves no gaffes,
good counting uses no tallies.
Good seals need neither locks nor bolts
yet leave no gaps and cannot be opened.
Good tying uses neither rope nor knot
yet cannot be undone.
Therefore the sage is good at saving people,
rejects nobody and no thing.
The good person is the bad person's teacher;
the bad person is the good person's raw material.
If you don't honor the teacher,
if you don't cherish the raw material,
your knowledge will only confuse you.
Call it Essential Wonder: mysterious, sublime.

TREKKERS RESPECTFUL of the wilderness pledge to leave no trace behind. This is difficult to do in our journeys in the wilderness of the world—especially if we also want to leave our imprint on the world before we die.

We leave many kinds of litter behind us. A thoughtless word can lodge in somebody's heart; a selfish action can scar a love. All our actions bear children. Is there a parent alive who does not regret something done while raising a child?

Some people are so fearful of the consequences of their actions they shut themselves away and try to not get involved. If you shut all the doors and windows of a house, though, the air goes stale. Other people are so fearful of gaffes they seek to eliminate all errors and exercise complete control; they usually break under the strain. Neither avoidance nor perfectionism can succeed in closing the gap between living and dying, being and nothingness.

Good living and right action are not virtuous or noble but simple and harmonious; they are the ordinary ways that naturally arise when we do not interpose our discriminating mind between ourselves and the needs of the moment.

Mindfulness cultivates this kind of wholeness. Mindfulness recently has become something of a prescriptive panacea; it's sometimes presented as a technique of maintaining attention in order to better obtain a desired result. This can be misleading. Mindfulness is not some special skill but a way to cultivate an awareness of your interbeing with the world's. It helps us see that our selves—and all around us—are not fixed but flowing. Mindfulness is neither prescriptive nor prohibitive. It just requires you greet all things in the world with equal love.

This sounds very appealing, doesn't it? But there is a catch: if we wish to accept all people (including ourselves) we must not reject anybody or anything (including ourselves). We must recognize that each of us has the potential to be any of us. The pedophile? There but for the grace of God goes I. The greedy polluter? I also am no stranger to lust and desire, to fouling my nest as well as the nest of others. To some extent I am able to restrain and transform these tendencies in myself; this is no cause for pride, but rather for gratitude—that the circumstances of my life have allowed me to turn this way and not that.

Practicing mindfulness in this fashion, everyone you meet is both your teacher and your student. Everything you do, think, say, or feel is the raw material you will digest and give back to the world in another form.

When you are able to cherish everything in the world as the raw material of yourself, and cherish everything in yourself as the raw material of the world, you save yourself and save others. This is Being: yourself. It is intimate and immediate, a miraculous activity that leaves no traces because it doesn't impose anything on anyone. It is the wonder of the Way actualizing itself through the mysterious vessel of each particular person.

Just this has space for all but leaves no gaps.

———

Raising our two daughters I studied the parenting manuals, talked with friends, consulted with psychologists, and worked with my wife to do the best possible job teaching them and nurturing them. Alas, I made many gaffes and left many traces that I'm afraid they will have to metabolize and transform. I sometimes cringe to see them struggling with a difficult residue I've bequeathed them.

It took me a while to realize my book knowledge and training as a psychologist was not very helpful. Ringing a mindfulness bell in the midst of a family dispute brought little peace if I didn't pay attention to the ever-evolving realities of my children rather than to my ideas about them. I had to learn to trust it was my daughters who would teach me how to parent.

Both my daughters are adults now. They sometimes ask me for advice. I usually don't really know what to say. So instead I just cherish them, trusting each one to realize herself. I feel honored to have the opportunity to watch their mysteries unfold and savor the sublime sense of wonder they inspire.

28

To know the male and abide by the female
is to be a river for the world.
Being a river for the world,
your ancient virtue constantly flows;
you return to your original face before you were born.
Knowing the mud is the lotus,
you are the pattern of the world,
the world's river valley.
Your eternal integrity is completely sufficient
without a hair's breadth's deviation.
You manifest fully, simple as uncarved wood.
When uncarved wood is cut to pieces,
it's turned into tools.
True masters are one with their tools;
truly great carving splits nothing up.

YOUR ORIGINAL NATURE is innocent as the wild grasses. Because you are innocent you do not have to be good, you need only be natural, in harmony with the self that exists prior to being shaped by reward and punishment.

Of course by the time you are reading this, you have been conditioned. Your original self, though, remains unconstrained by words and value judgments; it appears wherever you stop, transfixed by a sunset, and whenever laughter bubbles up without your quite knowing why. This unknowing innocence flows constantly: it cannot be stained, and its virtue is so basic to your fiber it cannot be lost.

The biblical story of Adam and Eve's Fall begins with each of them originally created perfect, then introduces the snake in the garden: sex. We have many ideas about sex, but basically sex is one of nature's methods for creating new forms of being. Sex turns separate souls into evolutionary opportunities, combining them in re-creation. In this way, sex is an antidote to the fragmentation and isolation of individuality.

We blossom by virtue of our bodies, natural to ourselves in our fundamental physicality. Cultural attitudes toward sexuality, though, muddy the water. Social pressures encourage us to present ourselves via a persona with an unambiguous gender identity; in these days of identity politics, you gain membership in a group by proclaiming your sexual proclivities. Celebrating a sexual (or, for that matter, an ethnic) identity can be a valuable way station on the path to liberation, but it's important not to seek personal integrity in a rigid identity that limits rather than frees you.

Male and female are not mutually exclusive; biologically, gender is a continuous not a dichotomous variable. Everyone has varying ratios of both testosterone and estrogen, and visible genitalia do not in themselves determine sexual identity. Gender is a result not just of genetics but also of your intrauterine experience and all that follows after. Whether your sexual preferences are exclusive or inclusive, you need not define yourself as bi, trans, hetero, homo, metro, or any other rigid category. Simply enjoy being, like everyone, a particular pattern of flesh and blood and skin and bones.

Of course you always manifest yourself through some specific form. Your skeletal structure is a personal variation of the human template, and your skin presents your unique features to the world. Your personality may lean more toward the extrovert or introvert, your sexual history may be creative, procreative, or virginal. Whatever form you take, though, it need not petrify you into your past nor split you off from possibility. Losing your virginity does not preclude you from being chaste the rest of your life any more than being abstinent assures you of remaining untouched. Being raped need not turn you into someone else's tool, so long as you do not close your heart to love.

At times we feel cut to pieces by our traumas, fragmented and broken, carved up into our different roles. We try to protect ourselves, but the masks we wear as shields distort our character into caricature. Your unconditioned self, though, cannot be grasped; because of this it cannot really be invaded, whittled down to some smaller size, or sliced fine into broken bits.

Your life flows over and under, around and through. Perhaps that's the formula with which you learned to tie your shoelaces. It is easy in our complicated lives to get tied into knots, tossed by the convolutions of events. Nevertheless, even when you are the material that is going over, under, around, and through, the fundamental string of your being remains itself. Loosen the knot, and it returns to its untwisted state, ready to take another shape.

It is not that there is no getting tangled up with problems or no release when your cares unravel; it is simply that throughout everything your fundamental nature remains whole.

———

One of my clients had been sexually abused as a child. She felt dirty, ashamed, besmirched—until one day she discovered something best expressed in her own words:

"I'm *me*," she said. "I'm not what *happened* to me."

Life is always moving; time is not linear, but lived. If you view yourself as an accumulation of the bits and pieces of your past, your experience becomes a prison. When you experience yourself as a shimmering potentiality, the pattern of your self becomes a prism, revealing the full spectrum of light.

29

Act on the world; try to control it.
You'll see it simply cannot be done.
The world is a spirit vessel;
it cannot be forced or treated as an object.
Manipulative action fails of itself;
clutching control, it slips from your grasp.
Things sometimes move forward, or follow behind.
Life blows hot and blows cold,
strong and weak, firm and soft,
getting on, getting off, rising up, falling down.
Sages let go of over-doing,
are not caught by extremes.
They live free from extravagant excess.

ON SOME LEVEL we feel we should be able to control the world at large and the world should cooperate with our efforts.

We make a kind of bargain with the world: "I can accept this much difficulty, but no more." If our car breaks down around the same time one of our children dies, it seems not only unfortunate but unfair, and we feel we have a right to be angry at the car, the mechanic, and the automaker. We think if we work hard at a task we should be rewarded, so if a hurricane destroys the house we saved up to buy we feel entitled to be depressed and look for someone to blame.

When we discover the cosmos is not necessarily interested in being benevolent to us personally, we tell ourselves "it's an unfair world." But the world is neither fair nor foul. Tsunamis, earthquakes, and volcanoes are natural occurrences, not insults to our human hubris. The world is not a thing that conforms to human values but the vast expanse in which our lives play out. You can travel through an expanse, you can experience it, you can furnish and decorate it, but since you cannot grasp it, you cannot control it.

Can we expect to control the world around us if we cannot even control ourselves? Examine the world of your body: you cannot treat it as an object. You cannot tell your blood how much oxygen to carry or dictate to your fingers how to hold a wine bottle by digitally instructing them of the number of pounds of pressure they should exert. You cannot force your body to stay young by micromanaging the number of times your heart beats each minute. There is a whole class of body functions—sleep, digestion, and so forth—where the more you command them, the more you block them. Screaming "RELAX!" at yourself during a panic attack is unlikely to have the desired effect.

While you cannot exercise complete control over your body's functions, you can influence them, and it's good to do whatever you can to nurture your health through diet and exercise. It's best, though, to do this for the enjoyment of eating good food and the pleasure of feeling your body move. If you expect whole grains and qigong to make you immortal you're likely to be disappointed.

The same holds true of your mind. Mindfulness consists of learning your mind is not an object to be managed. Try to think only one thought and your mind will wander; try to not think of something and your mind will turn to the elephant you attempt to not-think of. Thoughts, feelings, sensations, impulses, and consciousness move forward and back, bubbling up and sinking down.

Meditation is not a matter of controlling these ephemera but of accepting them while not acting on them. This gives them a larger space to wander in while you get out of the way: then they can find their own way, settle, and clarify. Meditation is letting go of self-centered control, "dropping" mind and body to cultivate the empty field where self-regulation comes forth naturally.

Western culture mistrusts self-regulation. The power of technology seduces us with the idea that we can control and regulate everything to our satisfaction. Intellectually, most of us recognize that nobody is in complete control of his life, but this doesn't stop us from trying to exercise control over not only ourselves but also over others: our parents, our children, our coworkers, even people we don't know, such as the drivers who pass us on the highway. When things don't go the way they "should" we become frustrated, angry, anxious, or depressed, depending on whether we blame ourselves, the other person, "the system," the gods, the stars, or fate.

The more you think you "should" be able to be in charge, the more you become addicted to control and vulnerable to the agonies of withdrawal when it breaks down. Addictions are sustained by thinking we can command things we cannot; it's not surprising, then, that AA gives a central place to the Serenity Prayer, seeking "to accept what cannot be changed, the courage to change what can be changed, and the wisdom to know the difference."

The Serenity Prayer was originally developed by the theologian Reinhold Niebuhr. Parts of it are well known, including its credo of taking life one moment at a time. Fewer people, though, are familiar with the portion of it that urges us to find serenity by "accepting hardship as a pathway to peace."

We tend to greet hardship as an obstacle to be overcome rather than as a path to peace. We strain ourselves if we put forth excessive, useless effort in the face of misfortune. When we greet difficulties not with extravagances of control, but by relaxing and letting go of overdoing, sometimes a small smile suffices to make room for ease.

———

On one Himalayan trek a friend of mine dropped his camera on a steep snow-covered hillside. As it bounced down the slope he rushed after it, endangering himself and others. He stopped, but the rest of the day and into the next he spent a considerable time loudly cursing his loss.

A few days later we were crossing a precarious wooden bridge with no sides or railings. One of the porters momentarily lost his balance and dropped his kit bag into the roaring rapids below. Like most Himalayan porters, he was poor; the bag contained many of his (few) worldly possessions. He paused for a moment, stared at the river, and then started laughing. His companions all joined in: how funny he looked when he lost his balance! What a splash the kit bag made from that height!

When we reached camp that night the crew all shared what they had with the kit-less porter. No one suffered any lack. Each of the Western trekkers slept alone, zipped up in a down bag in an individual tent. We had provided sleeping bags for each member of the crew, but the porters chose to cuddle together under a single blanket. Sharing each others' inner heat, their joined energies kept each other warm.

30

One who uses the Way to assist the ruler
doesn't use force of weapons to overpower the world.
Such violence doubles back on itself.
Where armies camp
brambles, thorns grow.
After great campaigns
bad years surely follow.
Able commanders achieve their results and that's all:
not using a win to gain personal power.
Achieve right results, but don't become arrogant;
achieve right results, but don't praise your deeds;
achieve right results because you have no choice.
This is achievement without using force.
If you're overdeveloped, this hastens decay.
This is far from right effort, astray from the Way;
lose the Way and you'll come to an untimely end.

WE ALL HAVE our favorite weapons. If you scorn those who love guns
and violent videogames, be aware scorn is your weapon of choice.

We arm ourselves in various ways. Some rely on words and wit; some
rely on fists and feet; some treat people as weapons to launch against
others. Anything can be a weapon: jokes, solicitude, memos, medication, meditation, tai chi, TV, ads, rumors, facts, mud, tree branches,

water, space heaters, refrigerators, cars, airplanes, bulldozers, hammers, poison, sweets, sound, silence.

Nothing is a weapon in and of itself: samurai swords can be works of art and plutonium can be a window to the science of the small. Though weapons vary in the hazards they present to us—it is easier to fall into violence if you have a gun in your hand—weapons are dependent on our intentions. They have no inherent identity except in how we employ them.

The problem is we are tempted by the illusion of power. The ability to cause physical, mental, or emotional harm is intoxicating because it temporarily banishes our sense of inadequacy and helplessness. In the heat of the moment, we tend to forget that exercising destructive power changes not only the object we're acting on, but us as well. Even in a "just" war like World War II, pilots who bombed cities suffered for the rest of their lives, either from conscious guilt or from the walls they erected within themselves against their memories. Soldiers returning from Vietnam, Iraq, and Afghanistan often bring back nightmares of violence that cause suffering for themselves, their friends, their spouses, and their children; these echoes of violence can reverberate for generations.

We often react to troubles by waging war against them. If you feel you can only overcome an obstacle by defeating and dominating it, then whether the difficulty is a person (an athletic competitor, a rival for a position), a predicament (a writing block, a physical weakness), or an internal conflict (approach, avoid), you are in a win-lose situation that is bound to cause you distress.

The Romantics made a virtue of struggle; they overvalued anguish as the source of inspiration. There's nothing wrong with anguish, but there's no great virtue to it, either. It's possible to tolerate troubles, solve problems, feel satisfaction, and move on without grim battles or triumphs that are glorious but exhausting. Crowing over a victory, if anyone notices, may earn you resentment as much as applause: if nobody notices, you may feel deflated and denigrate what you did achieve.

Force is spectacular but messy; fireworks burn out fast. When you accomplish your ends using an economy of means, this is not only elegant but will also leave you with more energy to devote to your next effort. The Way involves doing what is necessary to deal with a situation, but no more.

———

Meditators and spiritual seekers are not exempt from aggressive overdoing.

When I first started studying Zen the teacher gave us *koans* to sit with (*koans* are the traditional teaching stories of Zen, which stimulate the mind with conundrums that cannot be resolved through discursive thinking). Our teacher urged us all to put forth strenuous effort to overcome the koan as if it were an obstacle we needed to burst through. "Flare your nostrils!" he said. "You will never become enlightened if you don't flare your nostrils!"

We failed to notice how he laughed as he said this. We flared our nostrils and battled at the koan's gateless gate. I had some breakthroughs, but whenever I meditated sweat beaded my brow and my whole body shook with effort.

I went to a Zen temple in Japan. Monks there bragged about the number of koans they had solved and used this as a weapon to put down other monks. As a foreigner I was exempt from hazing but not exempt from feeling arrogant about my koan practice. The temple was freezing cold in more ways than one.

I left and for a while stopped Zen practice. I found some stillness meditating with the microcrystalline form of quartz Mount Diablo had granted me, but I still contended with my streams of pride and their cousin, fear of failure.

Some years later I was teaching on a Fulbright in India. Everything in my life was going well—my family was with me, we were all healthy and happy to be together; my work was interesting but not stressful, my Indian colleagues were warm and helpful—but somehow I didn't feel happy. Something was missing, but I didn't know what to do.

Lacking any clear path, I returned to zazen, but I felt aimless. Somehow it seemed that trying to solve koans would be using force to (over) develop myself. Fortunately I came across a book, *Returning to Silence*, which advocated sitting quietly, doing nothing. This form of meditation is called *shikantaza*, "just sitting." It felt very difficult and strange at first. It ran counter to my usual way of being. Probably for that reason, it turned out that sitting quietly, doing nothing, was precisely what I needed.

31

As for weapons—they're instruments of ill omen.
All natural beings abhor them.
One shuns them when walking the Way.
In peacetime the ruler honors the left;
in wartime the ruler honors the right.
Since weapons are evil, at best inauspicious,
a ruler employs them only when there's no other choice.
If wielding them, stays coolly unenthusiastic;
never prettifies them nor delights in their use.
To delight in weapons is to glorify killing.
Enjoy killing others, you'll never thrive in the world.
In joyful affairs one honors the left;
in mournful affairs one honors the right.
The lieutenant general stands to the left;
the supreme general stands to the right.
They arrange themselves as they would at a funeral.
When many have been killed in your battle,
honor them with your tears.
When you have won your battle,
mourn your victory with a wake.

SOME CONFLICTS are unavoidable. Even when we try to resolve disputes and seek harmony for discords, some disagreements are irreconcilable.

This is true for conflicts we experience within ourselves as well as for those we run into with other people.

There is no need to be afraid of conflict. Stirring the waters of disagreement can bring oxygen into an ecosystem; if you're not willing to sometimes make waves, you may end up with stagnant ponds. The important thing is not making nice nor maintaining calm, but facilitating flow. In doing this, whatever the nature of a dispute and its disputants, the truth is your friend.

Truth is not a thing, not an idea, but a living being. Truth is found not in facts but in the vital nature of changing circumstances that form and re-form to constitute the shifting realities of the playing field (or battlefield, as the case may be). One truth doesn't cancel out another: if you place competing truths side by side without favoring one and eliminating the other, you create an opportunity to integrate both into a new, three-dimensional vision.

So long as you do not get caught up in believing you own the One True Truth, battles need not lead to killing either beliefs or people. If you find yourself resorting to your favorite weapons to crush an opponent, though, you overstep to an extreme you may later lament. When you defeat an opponent it's best to feel sad about the necessity of vanquishing your foe and regret it if victory makes reconciliation impossible for the present. If you gloat you close off the possibility of future rapprochement; if your defeated opponents sense your sorrow, they may perceive a kinship in the echo of their own despair, and this can provide a doorway for a later mutually beneficial relationship.

Still, when life does come down to a contest between an irresistible this and an unmovable that, there will always be some loss. If two people in a dispute cannot find some larger, more encompassing vision, there will be the pain of people going their separate ways. When you make a personal choice to select one path and not another, there will be the pain of the road not taken. Either way, it is important to acknowledge the loss.

Whether your struggle is with conflicting impulses within yourself or with a challenging antagonist, when a battle results in one outcome rather than another allow yourself some grief for what is left unrealized. This will not only keep you from being overly invested in the direction you have chosen—which makes it easier to take a different tack should that be necessary in the future—but it also will open avenues of future enjoyment. You cannot know what the future will hold, but if you truly let go of the passing of one way of being at the time you make your choice, you'll be less likely to be dragged down by future remorse.

——

In high school and college I enjoyed theater. I worked as an actor, director, stage manager, and even wrote music for an off-Broadway production. I dreamed of the glories of being on stage and loved the crackle of excitement when the curtain went up.

There was a problem, though: I found I did not like the social environment of the theater world. Interpersonal interactions were often intense but short-lived, lasting no longer than production runs. Between the emotional jaggedness of the personal connections and the economic uncertainties of making a living in the theatre, I decided to pursue other careers.

Unfortunately, I did not take the time to adequately mourn my decision. Instead of grieving, I became depressed. Depression clings to what has been lost, whereas grieving lets it go.

I pretended I didn't "really" want to be in the theater, anyway. This was an angry falsehood I used to push myself on. I got over the depression, but it took me nearly a decade before I could enjoy a theatrical production: whenever I attended a play I could only see the opportunities I had denied myself.

Eventually I realized I was still looking for happiness in the applause of others for the roles I played, though now those roles were professional and family ones. I had to learn I am not the roles I play, to be happy being nothing special. As Shakespeare has Richard II say:

Thus play I in one person many people,
and none contented . . .
But whate'er I be,
nor I nor any man that but man is
with nothing shall be pleased, till he be eased
with being nothing.

32

The Way is timeless, nameless,
simple and natural, small and unassuming,
but no one can command it.
If rulers abided by the Way
it would be like they held a feast
with the world as their guest.
Heaven and earth would unite,
bestowing sweet rain.
By nature it would fall equally on all
with nobody giving orders.
Make distinctions:
set up systems, laws, institutions.
Then you have names.
Once there are names
you know it's time to stop.
If you know when to stop
you'll avoid trouble.
The Way in the world:
valley streams flow to rivers,
rivers flow to the sea.

•

WHEN YOU WAKE UP to this moment, you are newborn—innocent of before and after, each moment rests on a timeless silence. We need to listen to what the silence says before speech splits our infinities into rules.

It doesn't matter how much experience you accumulate, you will never be all-knowing and omnipotent. You were, are, and always will be a baby in comparison to the vastness of the universe. The parents of a newborn know it is the baby who rules the house, their schedule revolving around the baby's hunger and sleep. A baby's eyes, unblinking, drink in the world and us along with it as an ongoing feast.

You cannot command a baby. You can feed her, cradle her, and respond to her cries; you can coo and gurgle at her, change her diapers and feel the warmth of her cheek when you press your face to hers, but you cannot tell her what to do, or who to be. Does this make you love her any less?

Babies gradually learn to make distinctions: now is the time to eat; here is the place to go to the bathroom; work seriously before amusing yourself. We learn to eat when we're not hungry and make the marvelous ordinary by becoming productive rather than playful. We fill our minds with facts and line our mental space with laws.

Fortunately, having known not-knowing as a babe, no matter how sophisticated we become we cannot lose our essential capacity for wonder. What is sometimes called "the mind of clover" accompanies you throughout your life, unencumbered by excess baggage, able to respond equally to the novelty of the mobile over your crib, the lights of the aurora borealis, or the smile on the face of someone you love.

We try so hard to make something of ourselves, it's good to remember being yourself is as natural as flowing water. No matter how far water travels from its headwaters, it retains its basic nature. Innocent infant, knowing adult, dying elder: mountain stream, river rapids, estuary touching the sea: all water through and through.

We try so hard to be good adults. There's no need to push the river. It's fine to be respected for your adult accomplishments, but it will be your innocent joy that invites others to love you. In ruling yourself, be gentle caring for your infant; abiding by the Way, you don't need to give it orders. Staying simple, you can trust self-regulation to flow naturally.

———

We gave our daughter her first dish of ice cream when she was about eighteen months old. She tasted her first spoonful, smiled with delight, then attacked the ice cream enthusiastically. After she'd eaten about three-fourths of the ice cream in the dish she put down her spoon, smiled at us, and held out her arms to be taken out of her high chair. We hesitated: didn't she want to finish her ice cream? She shook her head "no" and smiled again. She had eaten as much as she wanted and knew how to stop.

When we get older we become less clear at listening to the signals of our body. Children try to stay up later so as not to miss anything; adults try to impose bedtime schedules with the force of law. One night we arrived at the airport with our four-year-old daughter only to learn our plane was delayed by several hours. We were dismayed; we had hoped our daughter would sleep on the plane and were anxious about how to manage her during the delay. It was nine o'clock in the evening, our daughter's usual bed time, so we thought we should coax her to go to sleep.

We sang to her, held her, rocked her, but to no avail. In a busy airport lounge, there was too much stimulation glittering for a little girl to allow herself to be lulled to sleep. After doing this for three hours we finally gave up around midnight. We told our daughter she could stay up as late as she wanted.

She stood up, laughed, and shouted enthusiastically: "I can stay up as late as I want!" She threw her arms out and began whirling around in a circle, repeating, "I can stay up as late as I want! I can stay up as late as I want! I can stay up . . ."

Around her fourth circle, in the middle of a sentence, her voice cut off: she abruptly fell asleep and collapsed to the ground. We caught her, tucked her in with her blankie, and held her. She slept soundly through the remainder of the delay and the plane flight that followed, self-regulated in sleep.

33

One who knows others is knowledgeable;
one who knows self is enlightened.
One who overcomes others has physical power;
one who overcomes self is strong.
One content with enough is truly wealthy;
one who acts resolutely has steady purpose;
one who abides in her true home endures.
One who dies but does not perish lives on.

YOU MUST KNOW YOURSELF to know the world.

Your thoughts, sensations, emotions, impulses, and awareness all color your experience; if you are familiar with your filters you may become less polarized when stressed. You gain increased freedom when you have the flexibility either to fix your eyes on an external object or to soften your gaze and, with your eyes still open, look deep within yourself. Your attention can be a wide or a narrow beam, scanning your surroundings or trained on a single point. Being aware of your modes of awareness allows you to fine-tune your focus. Your mind and body register your images of the world more sensitively than a camera; it helps to know how to adjust the opening and closing of your apertures, the speeds of your reactivities. You can adjust better to circumstances if you recognize you have a tendency to overexpose or a habit of introducing noise by excessive sharpening.

Knowing yourself requires you know not just what happens to you but your habitual tendencies to react a certain way. Awareness of your habits helps you inhabit yourself. The more you inhabit yourself, the more you'll find your home is not a matter of square footage but a sense of residing wherever you find yourself: more resonance than residence.

The more you feel at home in the world, the less you'll need to carry. With a lighter pack on your shoulders, it becomes easier to feel content. When you are content, you feel at peace.

You feel at peace when you have no unfinished business. When you have no unfinished business, dying is not so big a deal. When you die, if you leave no ghosts behind, you don't give up the ghost: you do not perish but pass on, and your going creates a pass for others to walk through.

———

My good friend and trekking companion Joel Schone died suddenly of a heart attack while leading a bicycle tour of the mountains of Ladakh. Born in America, when he was eight years old his family moved to England. He eventually became a schoolteacher there, but by the time he was forty he'd discovered he preferred hiking in the Himalayas to the security of a paycheck. He left his teaching job and devoted the last fifteen years of his life to leading groups of people on treks in Ladakh and Nepal.

He made no money from his trips. He had no fixed home. He gave of himself completely, taking his payment in joy from the happiness he saw in others' faces as they wandered the high deserts and snowy peaks.

He knew what he was doing. He told me he was aware that, without health insurance or pension, he might die younger than others of his cultural background, but he was willing to risk this because he was doing what he loved. He felt that was enough.

I miss Joel, but he is right: his life was, is, and will be enough. His friends continue on trails he widened by his walking.

34

The Way flows easily, vast;
omnidirectional streams left or right.
All live by its grace, and it accepts all.
All entrust themselves to it but give it no name.
It accomplishes its tasks but makes no claims for itself;
it nourishes ten thousand things but does not lord over them.
Without desire, with no self-centered needs,
it can be called small.
Though all depend on it, the Way does not covet control;
it can be called great.
Not trying to accomplish great things,
true greatness is realized, vastness itself.

GREATNESS CAN BE FOUND everywhere, since it is not a matter of accomplishment.

A newborn baby is great in wonder, vast in both her vulnerability and her potential. Her gaze wanders easily here and there, treats everything as equally fascinating but lingers lovingly on her parent's face.

There is something in each of us that yearns for greatness. Infants have no particular goal in mind, so initially they grow innocently into agents of their future selves, but soon they turn into young children aiming for adulthood. Ask any five-year-old what she wants to be when she grows up: whether it be firefighter or police chief, president or rock star, children want to be bigger than they are. They have learned to compare themselves to others and with that loss of innocence taste both grandiosity and humiliation. This is the psychology of narcissism, a strand of self-development distinct from the ego's lessons of reward and punishment. We wish to be admired as well as loved; they are not the same thing.

You will overidealize some of the people you love, and then they are bound to disappoint you by being sometimes merely human. How you cope with this will depend, in part, on how you feel about being merely human yourself. This in turn will depend in part on how the people you looked up to were able to tolerate it when they (inevitably) failed to live up to your expectations—which will be a function of their own past interpersonal experiences.

Your needs for admiration and love form one link in a long chain of being, of successes and failures, acclaim and neglect, hurt and healing, all arising from our inevitably self-centered needs. Seeking to satisfy these needs, people make claims on us and we make demands on ourselves, but it is impossible to always satisfy all demands. If you are not able to accept the fact that sometimes you will let others and yourself down, you may be prone to feel that whatever you accomplish and whoever you may be is not "enough."

There is something in us that does not easily settle for enough; we want not just to *have* more but also to *be* more: more powerful, more invulnerable, to be the ultimate exemplar of some cherished dream. We may secretly fear we won't be truly "enough" unless we reach a pinnacle of achievement: to be the quarterback in the Super Bowl, to win a MacArthur "genius" award, to be the first woman president, a movie star, the Dalai Lama, or Mother Teresa. Realistically you know your chances for this are slim, but on some nagging irrational level you might feel that if you don't reach a comparable height, you will be less than great. This mistakes greatness for fame and power: don't be misled by false illusions of what greatness consists of, or you might start to feel being yourself means settling for less.

Stop comparing yourself to others. Being yourself is not a matter of big or small; whatever heights you reach are uniquely yours and therefore incomparable. Only that which is incomparable is truly great.

The question is not how you can become great: the question is how you can realize being greatly yourself. The paradox is that to fully realize yourself you must let go of self-centered striving and acknowledge your personal accomplishments rest on something greater than yourself. Then you can depend on the grace you have been granted.

———

In Kathmandu the sole of one of my sneakers became detached from the toe box. I found a shoe repair shop in an alley where a *dalit*, a member of the so-called "untouchable" caste of India, was squatting in a small alcove, surrounded by scraps of old shoes and a few tools of his trade. I gave him my shoe, pointing to the problem.

I expected he'd slap some glue on, press it together, give it back to me and ask for his pay. Instead he examined it carefully and worked on it meticulously. He started by pulling the sole further off the shoe, then sanded and smoothed both surfaces. He applied a first layer of adhesive to make it tacky, let it dry partially, applied a second layer, achieved a good seal, tapped it with a little hammer, then clamped it. After it dried he smoothed the edges with a file and skillfully made little adjustments with brushes, awls, and other tools I did not recognize. He spent about an hour doing a superb repair rather than the slapdash patch I'd expected. He could have easily taken advantage of a naive foreigner but charged me just a few rupees for his work as a master craftsman.

Weeks later I had a stroke in the Himalayas. I somewhat unwisely insisted on limping out, accompanied (and sometimes carried by) a young sherpa. After about a week of this my symptoms started to get worse. My sherpa guide became anxious, but we finally reached a sizable village. I saw him scanning the market stalls for a place to stay when his face lit up with relief and delight.

"Mama-san," he called out, and an elderly woman with Tibetan features emerged from the darkness of her shop and greeted him. They chatted animatedly for a few minutes, then she took me in. I asked my companion if she were a relative: he replied no, but every sherpa knew of Mama-san. She and her family had escaped from Tibet in 1960, and she had long been known for taking in travelers in need.

I stayed with her several days in her two-room hut. She was very poor but shared whatever she had with me, as she did with whoever came to her in need. She had two young girls living with her. They were not her children or any relative to her; when I asked why she was taking care of them she replied, "Nobody else was." Each morning she'd rise early and chant Buddhist mantras while lighting candles at her altars. She'd cook breakfast, help her girls get ready for school, send them off, and then open her shop.

She had lost everything when she fled Tibet. Her son had died in a fire; her elderly husband had to be away for half the year working on caravans in the salt trade. I asked her if she was angry at the Chinese for forcing her to leave her home and she replied no, she just hoped they too could find peace.

With all respect for my root teachers, when I think of a great bodhisattva, an embodiment of compassion for all beings, I think of Mama-san; when I think of a great Zen practitioner, giving full attention to what's right in front of him, I think of the shoe repairman in Kathmandu.

35

Hold up the Clear Mirror,
the whole world comes.
Beyond harm, safe, serene,
content being one.
When tasty dishes and songs are offered,
passersby stop.
When the Way speaks, though, it's bland,
plain, no special flavor.
When looked at, no thing to see.
When listened to, no thing to hear.
When used, no thing to use up.
Hence, inexhaustible.

You ARE A MIRROR to the world, reflecting all you experience. How could you not be a mirror of the world? You respond to everything you encounter. Being truly yourself, you respond to everything as truly itself.

When clear skies come, a clear sky is reflected; when a thunderstorm comes, a thunderstorm is reflected. Your mouth waters at the smell of baking bread. A friend's leg is smashed, and you wince: a baby smiles, and you melt. You are the breath of the world, sometimes a sigh and sometimes a silly giggle.

Depending on your skills and experiences you may or may not have your uses; because there is no other person quite like you, you are quite literally "un-*use*-ual," a clear mirror that can never be used up. You, along with every one and every thing, are inherently a reflecting being, and thus intrinsically luminous.

You may think that if you are a mirror, you are a very smudged and dirty one. You may be frustrated at the distortions that inevitably accumulate in your meetings with the world, but this does not change the nature of the looking glass with which you see. Dust may alight on the surface of a mirror, but the mirror's basic nature is unchanged. Mirrors are windows on the world and, as Shunryu Suzuki Roshi said, we don't clean the windows because they are dirty: we clean them to reveal how clear they essentially are.

No effort, no psychotherapy, no spiritual practice can make you into anyone other than who you are. They cannot even make you be more like yourself; you are completely yourself each moment.

Being a mirror, you do not need to be special. Every mirror faces the world from a different angle and reflects different facets of the whole. Just as you are a mirror to the world, the world is a mirror to you. Walk on the beach, and the sand reflects your footsteps. Speak kindly to a dog, and it will wag its tail. Plant green lawns in the desert, and you will go thirsty.

When you and the world meet, you are two mirrors facing each other. Reflecting reflections break into an infinity of pieces, each of which is its own mirror. There is no end to this and no beginning. It is inexhaustible.

———

When I first began working as a therapist, I thought clients needed to have their symptoms interpreted to them. I didn't put much faith in plain, unvarnished reflective listening. Gradually I learned to trust that it is clients, not therapists, who make therapy work. Our voice sounds different to us heard through the bones of our ears than when we hear ourselves on a recording; our words sound different to us when they are said back to us by someone else.

The eye cannot see itself. We are not the images we hold of ourselves. Even when using a mirror we see only an image, one that reverses right and left.

One of my clients, a young woman, once said:

"When you can see yourself in others' eyes—that sure beats a mirror."

36

What is gathered in must first be scattered,
what is weakened must first be strengthened.
What is toppled must first be raised,
what is taken must first be given.
This is called the subtle illumination within what is evident:
the soft and weak overcome hard and strong.
Fish shouldn't be taken out of the watery depths.
A state's sharp weapons should not be displayed.

To BE YOURSELF you must reach beyond yourself, stretching your boundaries to make friends with the unacknowledged strangeness within and around you. Even the simplest single-celled amoeba stretches out pseudo-pods, temporary extensions of itself it sends out to interact with the unfamiliar, bringing novel material back into the cell and reassembling itself anew.

Falling apart is necessary to coming back together. If the double helix of our DNA did not break down into separate strands, our genes could not transcribe their messages. For families to enjoy healthy reunions, they must allow their individual members to stray: if there is no wandering, how can there be a coming home?

It's hard to trust to your wholeness without having the experience of going through a breakdown and surprising yourself by surviving. It's not possible to become strong without exercising your muscles to tiredness. If you wish to abolish a bad habit, suppressing it just leaves it lurking to surprise you at an inopportune time; if you bring the habit out into the light by intentionally exposing it in a way that is safe but not reinforcing, it will gradually extinguish.

Do you wish to be loved? First learn to love others with no thought of return. To do that, you need to also love the rejected and hidden portions of yourself.

The best way of discovering your unacknowledged selves is in interactions with others. Let others see you: everyone has a different perspective on you from the way you see yourself, so reflecting on those reflections gives you added depth. Reciprocate by seeing others without imposing your ideas of how they "should" be.

"Shoulds" are weapons we wield to insulate ourselves from the messy realities of inter-being. When we array our "shoulds" we substitute "ought" for "is"; this can get in the way of appreciating our different states. When you drop the "shoulds" and show yourself without artifice while seeing others without blurs, you illuminate both yourself and them.

Our lives are deep in paradox: attempting to eliminate our contradictions can leave us drowning on dry land. All life exists only in relationship: the quick with the still, the living with the dead. The inorganic elements are the building blocks for organic growth.

I once asked my Zen teacher, Mel Weitsman, what I should tell people who asked, after he died, what his teaching consisted of. He thought a long time, and finally said, "When I forget myself, I find myself."

———

One way of "forgetting yourself to find yourself" is to plunge so wholeheartedly into your activity there is no longer any separation between actor and action. Another way is to intentionally do something you've previously regarded as "not me." This is a common method in Bowenian therapy, which aims to widen your sense of who you are by having you identify a pattern in your family of origin and then act in ways that contravene it.

Early in my Bowenian training I became aware of the following family pattern: my mother was overweight and had high blood pressure so she frequently went on a diet. At the end of dinner my mother would serve dessert to my father and me but have none herself. My father would take a spoonful of his chocolate pudding, hold it out to my mother, and say "Have some!" My mother would protest, "Don't tempt me, I'm on a diet!" and I would chime in, "Dad, it's not good for her." My father would then say, "Ah, you don't know how to live and enjoy yourself."

My Bowenian therapist coached me, the next time I went back home, to side with my father instead of my mother. I protested if I did this I wouldn't be true to myself, since I didn't agree with my father. My therapist said that wasn't the point, the point was to get out of my habitual pattern and stretch myself.

So the next time I was in the situation where my father tantalized my mother with a fattening dessert and my mother protested, I said what I had carefully rehearsed: "Well, Mom, Dad has a point. Why not enjoy yourself sometime?" As I said this, I was flooded by anxiety. I felt as if I were killing my mother, hastening a heart attack or stroke.

But then something odd happened: First, I realized my father *did* have a point: some people choose to indulge and live a shorter life. Second, I realized that my mother was a grown woman who could make up her own mind. She didn't need me to be her ally in her dealings with my father.

This was a tremendous relief. Liberated from my automatic reactions and thoughts of what each of us "should" do in this situation, I felt a sense of freedom. By raising a different possibility than I was used to, my sense of being trapped in everyone's predefined expectations dissolved.

I found I could interact with my parents as myself, not as my role in a family drama. This enabled me to begin to see my parents as real people rather than characters in a role-play. I began to experience a more authentic, truly loving (if more unpredictable) relationship with each of my parents, and with myself as well.

37

Tao everlasting does not act
yet nothing is left undone.
If rulers could abide by it,
people and all things would transform by themselves.
If in transforming desire stirred,
nameless simplicity would grace them with stillness,
natural as uncarved wood.
Settled in stillness by nameless simplicity,
heaven and earth right themselves naturally.
Free from desire's hindrance,
all self-orders itself.
The world is at peace.

EVERY MOMENT you are completely yourself. There's no way to avoid being yourself; no way to augment it; no way to blot out any portion of what you experience. Matter and energy can be converted but never destroyed: were any instant of your life to be erased, the entire universe would cease to be.

You realize yourself moment by timeless moment. You become yourself, not in the sense of developing from not-self to real-self, but in the same way an ornament shows off its wearer to advantage. You are becoming to yourself.

When you are a child, you do this being fully yourself as a child mewling and puking in your nurse's arms; as an elder, you do this being fully yourself sans teeth, sans eyes, sans taste, sans everything. As your own ruler, you govern yourself as best you can; as your own servant, you can discern how to serve by settling down into the immediacy of being present. Someone calls and you answer, "Here I am."

It doesn't matter what you think: all thoughts are bubbles of your self's concepts.

It doesn't matter what you feel: all emotions are forms of your feeling your Way.

It doesn't matter what you sense: whether you are blind or keen-sighted, five-fingered or an amputee, musical or tone-deaf. The doors of perception can only offer an illusory approximation of Reality, but they are still the gateless gates of *your* reality.

It doesn't matter what you do. When you idle away a day flying a kite, you manifest yourself with the wind. When you work late or party until dawn, fail a test or find your love, these are simply different flavors. Straying from your path, each stumble is a halfway house to recovery.

You may feel shattered into pieces but silently, deeply, you are always self-ordered and at peace. You right yourself naturally; rest follows exertion, after sorrow comes happiness.

Yet often we say, "I don't feel like myself today." Who, then, are you feeling like? When you feel "I'm not myself" it is a sign that something doesn't sit right. Desire has entered in; you wish to be other than you are or wish the world to be other than it is. At such moments, you can run over, under, or around the experience, but the only way to genuinely restore Rightness is *through*.

In this journey you are never alone. The sky always covers you, the earth always upholds you; you find yourself at the horizon where they meet. You are touched by all you touch, your source and your frontier weaving together. Being yourself, you are strenuous and upright, but at the same time easily contented and joyous.

Meditation is basically simple and natural—what could be easier than "sitting quietly, doing nothing"?—and meditation retreats are usually held in plain settings designed to foster the calm and quiet of nameless simplicity. Nevertheless, we human beings are able to complicate our lives even in the most undemanding of settings, dealing with the most straightforward of instructions.

Anyone who has meditated for a while is likely to go through times when it seems impossible to settle down and nothing feels right. Some struggle with physical discomfort; others have to deal with intense feelings of anger, anxiety, or depression that come unbidden. The swirls of past traumas and future fears may make it difficult to abide in stillness. In the protected environment of the meditation hall it is hard—though not impossible—to blame others for your current unhappiness, and looking at the people all around you sitting quietly it is easy to believe everyone else is experiencing deep peace except yourself.

By temperament and conditioning I grew up inclined to restless action and unquiet complexity; I've found it hard to keep my mouth shut and rarely met a simple situation I couldn't make more difficult by overthinking it. Although I yearned to find some peace of mind, "sitting quietly, doing nothing" was difficult for me. I experienced a long stretch (several years, actually) during which nearly every moment of meditation seemed like hell. Physical pain wracked my body while emotional pain overwhelmed me. Waves of sadness, tears, and rage often welled up, but for no apparent reason. I could not get a grip on them, nor loosen their grip on me.

I didn't understand. During one retreat's public question-answer session I asked my teacher Sojun, "WHAT IS THIS?" and he answered with a single word:

"Nirvana."

I experienced a jolt of shock, but also of waking up; though I did not understand it, in some mysterious fashion beyond discursive thinking, in the midst of my difficulties "Nirvana" felt true and right. This encouraged me but didn't translate into any change in my experience of meditation practice, so I continued to struggle.

Since zazen encourages sitting still, sometimes I tried to sit absolutely motionless; I'd become rigid and the pain intensified. Since Sojun describes continuously making subtle adjustments during zazen, sometimes I'd notice whatever came up, soften around it, and smile at it—the hurt persisted. I tried accepting whatever came up and letting go; the hurt might ebb briefly, but it returned promptly. I tried going deeper into the pain, I tried dedicating whatever suffering I endured to the benefit of all beings; still the hurt came back time and time again, more and more intense, sometimes overwhelming me.

One day I had a practice interview with my friend Alan Senauke and described everything I had tried and how nothing worked. Alan looked at me and said, "Bob, you don't get it. Don't *do* anything!"

Ah. Here I got a hint of *wu wei*, "doing nondoing." Being still doesn't mean not moving, and not-doing invokes freedom of flow, not repression. Trust is the key to allow all to settle and transform.

A short while later on a trip to southern Spain I took an easy afternoon walk to the summit of an 11,413 foot peak. I relaxed under the bright blue empty sky. The wind blew chill across the upper slopes, but the Andalucian plains were warm below. A little tendril of white suddenly condensed out of the air, just beyond my reach, appearing from nowhere, swirling and shimmering. Just as suddenly it evanesced, vibrant in vanishing. Another transient strand of insubstantial cloud sprang into being and disappeared.

Here it was clear: empty stillness is ever moving. All the weather of our lives shows us the Way self-ordering itself. The world is at peace by virtue of its spinning whirl.

Part II: Te ～ Rightness

Te is sometimes translated as "virtue," sometimes as "power," but it transcends dualistic judgments of right/wrong, good/bad. Te is how the Way is expressed through a rightness that emerges to accord with circumstances naturally, "just so."

38

High virtue isn't virtuous,

thus it truly has virtue.

Low virtue never frees itself from virtuousness,

therefore it has no true virtue.

A person of highest virtue takes no action,

has no private ends to serve.

A person of lower virtue puts forth effort,

having many causes to act.

A highly humane person acts

without any particular end in mind.

A highly righteous person acts

for many justifiably good reasons.

A person of high propriety acts

and when no one responds

rolls up his sleeves and forces people to comply with the rituals.

So when the Way is lost,

that's when we resort to virtue.

When virtue is lost,

that's when we resort to humaneness.

When humaneness is lost,

that's when we resort to morality and righteous justice.

And when righteous justice is lost,

that's when we resort to ceremonies of propriety.

Ritual ceremonies? Mere husks of sincere faith,

marking the beginning of confusion and disorder.
Foreknowledge is a blossomy ornament of the Way,
the beginning of delusion.
The true person
relies on the heart not the husk,
the fruit not the flower,
leaves that for *just this.*

THERE IS NO VIRTUE in being yourself, only vivacity.

If you are attached to thinking of yourself as a virtuous person you can easily feel threatened when other people question your motives, criticize or disagree, or thwart your good intentions. If you aspire to be a good person, you risk the pitfall of thinking you are not good enough—in which case you may turn your anger and despair inward or project it out onto others.

Just being human is enough; it connects you to everyone else in your shared flawed humanity. Living is not a quest for brownie points or gold stars. You don't need a reason to exist, any more than you need a reason to defend your liking for ice cream that is chocolate rather than vanilla. As soon as you feel a need to justify yourself you become trapped in right and wrong. If you convince yourself your beliefs are righteous you may be inclined to proselytization, and from there it's a short step to inquisition, earthquakes, and executions.

Instead of striving to conform to some moralistic ideal, you can just be your ordinary self and accord with whatever the circumstances demand of you. If you try to make circumstances fit your ideology rather than the other way around you may become frustrated; you may use excess force to try to make things go the way you think they "should" be and exhaust yourself.

There is no need to prop yourself up by being proper. In popular parlance: be real. The gateway to compassion doesn't hold people to some ideological standard but recognizes all being has its function and place. Prescriptive moral codes and restrictive laws are usually prejudices clothed in moral majorities: they provide justifications but not justice.

The truth of your being is not a matter of being correct in ceremonies of yourself. Your true person is not somewhere far away but always present: it is the gift of your presence fully bestowed right here, right now.

———

When I first began Buddhist practice, I thought I would be more virtuous and a better parent, husband, and psychotherapist if I didn't let my feelings get the better of me. When provoked I would take several deep breaths, put irritation aside, smile gently, and calm down. I was fairly successful in this, at least on the surface, but I suspect I came across to others as artificial and perhaps more than a bit sanctimonious.

At that time my daughters were five and nine years old. As any parent knows, children often push their parents to the edge of their tolerance to test their boundaries. Perhaps because I grew up in an environment where my parents fought a great deal and were sometimes out of control in their anger, I made a special effort to remain even-tempered with my children.

One day my nine-year-old daughter was particularly provocative. I teetered on the edge of "losing it" and yelling but managed to catch myself. I took a deep breath and in a level voice tried to respond with measured if somewhat artificial "active listening." My daughter looked me in the eye, stamped her foot, and cried:

"Dad! A kid has to be able to make her father mad!"

She was right. I had been offering her only the husk of parenting. Not getting angry was not being real.

If there are no mad fights, there are no opportunities for reconciliation. Making up is one of the delights of love.

39

Originally these realized oneness:
the sky, being one, is clear;
the earth, being one, is stable;
the spirits, being one, are animated;
the valleys, being one, are replenished;
the ten thousand things, being one, manifest themselves;
the rulers, being one, are sovereign.
But from this we can infer:
if the sky were only clear it would shatter;
if the earth were only stable it would crack;
if the spirits were only animated they would fade;
if the valleys were only replenished they would stagnate;
if the ten thousand things only manifested themselves they
    would become extinct;
if the rulers were only sovereign they would be cast down.
The exalted depends on the humble,
the high depends on the low for its foundation.
So kings and queens profess to be orphaned:
insignificant, poor, and unworthy.
Is this true humility?
But when they have many carriages and just say they have none—
not wanting to glitter like jade
they *clunk* like stones.

WE WANT TO FEEL whole. We yearn to feel we belong, that we are part of some larger entity, that there is some unifying fabric to our lives.

At heart you are fundamentally whole. Your very yearning is a sign of this: you could not long for a rejoining if you did not have some basic sense of originally being in a harmonious union.

Most of us have experienced moments of feeling this oneness. Perhaps it has occurred on an autumn field open to the sky with the few remaining leaves on the trees bearing witness to the cycles of the seasons. Perhaps it has occurred during a lazy moment on a warm beach whose sands were baked still for a moment as they entertained the constant calls of winds and waves. Perhaps it was at the birth of a child or the funeral of a friend or relative. Perhaps you simply got out of bed one morning and everything clearly proclaimed its place; you saw your larger self reflected in the smile of someone you love or even in the aroma of a cup of coffee urging you to wake up.

These experiences remind us of our true home, and we want our awareness of this to go on forever. It's wonderful to feel firmly planted, vigorous yet still, stable yet vital. If we try to hold on to these states they turn rancid, but when we lose touch with them we often feel we are missing something, isolated, or lost.

When you feel you are lacking some quality or have lost some precious essence, your thinking seeks some concrete trait and your heart wants to embrace some solid object to confirm yourself. Your being, though, can only be experienced as ungraspable flow. If you look around, you see the universe shimmers in ebbs and flows, constantly breathing the ins and outs of being.

When you feel you are missing something, that in itself is a complete experience. Being stymied is also part of the Way, the intimate counterpart of flowing. According to Chuang Tzu:

> The men of ancient times who had attained the Way were happy if they were blocked in, and happy if they could get through . . . Being blocked or getting through are no more

than the orderly alternation of cold and heat, of wind and rain.

Being mindful doesn't mean being always clear-minded; being composed doesn't mean being always in control. Eihei Dogen, the founder of Soto Zen in thirteenth-century Japan, said that being enlightened means realizing that 80 percent of the time you're deluded.

You don't have to do anything special except to stop pretending. Most of us have experienced how the false facade we strain to maintain develops stress fractures if it is at odds with our actual experience. Sometimes we pretend we're big and strong, and hide our frailties. Sometimes we pretend to be small and weak, and hide our power. Faced with a painful event, we may be tempted to sidestep a challenge with its attendant risk of failure, try to avoid blame by denying our responsibility—"it's not my fault!"—or adopt the role of a helpless victim of circumstances. The danger here is we may convince even ourselves of our helplessness.

Whether it is a trait, an idea, a role, or a feeling, whenever we become attached to just one side of a matter, we become one-dimensional. Searching for a false stability we cling to illusions that our transient states are permanent traits and get stuck in our protests and pretensions. In reality we are all both weak *and* strong, broken *and* whole. To pretend otherwise is to stop ringing true.

When you stop pretending to be other than you are, when you stop pretending the world is other than it is, your life becomes unstuck: a continual procession, the play of hide and seek, unfinished and complete, universal and particular.

⎯

I met a friend outside the Zen center who I knew had been having some family troubles. I asked him how he was doing. My friend paused, reflected, and sighed.

"From the absolute point of view," he said, "everything is just as it must be."

I smiled.

"From the relative point of view," he continued, "things could be better."

I gave him a hug.

40

The Tao moves by returning,
functions by weakness.
The ten thousand things' source is being,
sometimes called life and death;
Being's source is nonbeing,
beyond life and death.

RETURNING HAS GOTTEN a bad name, as if it were somehow a retreat or retrogression. You return an item to the store if it is flawed or unwanted; if you return to where you started you may be ridiculed for going in circles. We forget there is a power inherent in circles, which have a center but no beginning and no end.

Modernity worships progress: onward and upward. The idea of progress is relatively new; for most of human history people expected daily life to be the same for their children as it was for their parents' parents' parents. Now novelty has become the norm, and we say familiarity breeds contempt. The most familiar relationships in our lives—our families—can easily look uninteresting compared to the shiny allure of what's new downtown.

Capitalism encourages the consumption of "new and improved" instead of "tried and true" because it depends not on just making a profit but on creating ever-increasing profits to attract investors. "Growth and more growth" becomes the mantra not just of economics but also a model for personal aspirations: if you're not constantly improving yourself, you may worry it's a sign something is wrong with you.

It's exhausting to move always onward. If you don't ever rest by returning to yourself in stillness you will need more and more stimulation from your environment to keep going, like the ions in particle accelerators that need bigger and bigger charges from electromagnets to keep boosting their speed as they go further and faster. This kind of linear progression is ultimately unsustainable. In particle physics, going faster makes you heavier, so it becomes harder and harder to increase your velocity.

We are biological beings, not particles. Biology does not function in straight lines but in exuberant branchings; the limbs of the evolutionary tree grow not just upward but out. Axons of even a single nerve in your brain grow in tangled connections more complex than the most ambitious electrical wirings of engineers.

Biological organisms' lives are healthy when they follow cyclical rhythms rather than escalating spirals. Healthy organisms do not go ever onward but function by well-regulated feedback in rhythms that expand and contract; every living being's actions return to itself as it touches the worlds within and without in an ongoing process of adaptation to shifting circumstances. The cells in our body need to strike a balance between dying and regenerating: if a single cell goes on and on reproducing itself, we don't call that productive growth, we call it cancer. If a person keeping going and going and stays up many nights in a row, it causes serious symptoms; the more regular our sleep cycle the more restorative it is.

We need to refresh ourselves by returning to our source to rest in nonbeing. Refreshment, though, these days comes marketed in the form of energy drinks that advertise their ability to jolt you into being more productive (heaven forbid you should be so unproductive as to take a nap) and video games that promise to provide brain stimulation to keep you from ever stagnating. Computer networks even let us play these games with others around the world so we need never feel alone.

Our inherent interconnectedness, though, does not depend on DSL or wi-fi but on a way of being intimate with the world, a form of love.

Love reaches beyond itself, touching the source that supports both self and other. This source is not "inside" or "outside" you or me; it is some deeper fold in the reality of being that encompasses both going and coming, birth and death, departures and returns.

———

The source of yourself is not you, but if you do not return to yourself, you will never find it. All meditations are basically a matter of returning to yourself. You might want to sample this by doing the first and last movements of Dayan ("Wild Goose") Qigong:

Stand with your feet shoulder width apart, parallel to each other. Relax; let the weight of the body distribute itself evenly between both feet. Keep your eyes open but with a soft focus that doesn't peer out, but instead gazes within.

Let your arms hang by your sides. Relax your wrists and hands; let your fingers spread. Then turn your palms out and slowly gather your-self to yourself by raising your arms shoulder high and in a continuous motion encircling your *qi* (energy) by bending your arms and elbows. Draw the energy or calm you've gathered in toward you by bringing your palms to your forehead.

With the palms of your hands still facing your body, let your hands slowly sink down at their own pace, following with your mind within the body as the hands descend until they reach the level of your navel.

Pause. Let everything settle. Then let the hands come the rest of the way down to your sides. Bring your feet together.

Having returned to yourself where you are, resume your regular activities, refreshed.

41

When the ablest students hear the Tao
they practice it, and just barely are able to keep
    to its center.
When middling students hear the Tao
they hear it but don't hear it; are sometimes on it,
    sometimes off.
When the dullest students hear the Tao
they laugh out loud.
If they didn't laugh
it wouldn't be the Way.
The old sayings go:
the bright path seems dark,
the path forward seems to go backward,
the level path seems bumpy,
high virtue seems a deep gorge,
great whiteness seems mottled,
abundant virtue seems insufficient,
staunch virtue seems timid,
genuine truth seems dubious.
The great square has no corners,
the great vessel is incomplete,
the great sound is ever so faint,
the great form is shapeless.
The Tao is ungraspable and nameless.

It alone renders help and fulfillment.
Beginningless, endless,
good beginning, good end.

You cannot find your way by hearing it from somebody else.

Sermons can be seductive, but since they're just words, they make misleading teachers. Ultimately you must create your path yourself by walking it. At a certain point you must discard everything you have learned, everything you have been told, and take a foolish-wise step back to your true self shorn of any markers or external guidance.

I needed to do this after I suffered a stroke in the Himalayas, when I struggled for a while to find my way. I grappled with the fact that none of the "-isms" I had clung to—Buddhism, Taoism, Marxism, liberalism—were going to rescue me from life and death. Psychotherapy, qigong, meditation, neuropsychology, eating "right," and trying to be "good" all paled in the face of the raw existential reality of being a vulnerable human who was going to die. Nothing could save me from being myself, whatever that might be: I might as well live any way I wanted to.

I spent a year reviewing my life and considered all options. Why not have my short life be self-centered, ruled by hedonism, living solely for my own comfort and pleasure? I couldn't find anything wrong with that, but somehow it just didn't seem to suit me; I've tasted the fruits of that path and found them either too rich for my taste or to sour quickly. I stumbled about (literally as well as metaphorically, since the stroke had affected my balance) searching for what could provide a basis for my life and came up with four foundations:

I felt I had to start with truth, with seeing things as they are. Truth is not some thing to cling to, since it is always changing, but truth is not merely relative: it is what is really real once we remove all personal filters and preferences. I don't see any particular virtue in truth—it's simply easier than falsehood. Starting from false premises by even small degrees soon leads you far astray. So even though I can't really free myself from all my filters nor point to what "the truth" is, I've adopted the motto "the truth is your friend."

Once I was committed to living with truth, I needed to acknowledge that from the standpoint of personal preference I don't like many of the truths I see: injustice, illness, death, violence, the self-centered stupidity of partisan politics and power. Within myself I sometimes discover selfish pride, greed, sexual fantasies, narcissism, sloth, fear, depression, anger. When I encounter any of these I feel pain. Although sometimes I can find a solution for a particular situation, I know another problem is sure to follow. In the absence of any universal anodyne I could find only one "answer" to the inevitable aches and sorrows inherent in existence: somehow, compassion arises.

When the world hurts inside and out, when white seems mottled and goodness insufficient, compassion seems to soften the blows as I (together with everyone else) am knocked about by life. Compassion helps remind me we're all in this together. For me it is a necessary response, one that arises naturally from some deep I-know-not-where to ease our suffering.

Having settled on truth and compassion, I found myself smiling in amusement; I realized I was being very serious about all this. Finding wholeness in my incompleteness was squaring the circle and inherently humorous. A good guffaw seemed as effective as therapy or meditation for stopping excess thinking and increasing my enjoyment of the world. The air bubbles of laughter provide leavening so that truth and compassion have room to rise.

It took some time and a friend's suggestion to help me realize I needed one more ingredient for my life. Flour of truth, water of compassion, yeast of laughter: they work pretty well together, but the dough still requires that we knead it into some shape. Beauty emerges when we shape our paradoxes of being into elegant, appropriate forms; I discovered I need beauty almost as much as I need bread. Fortunately, we can find beauty everywhere.

Truth, compassion, laughter, beauty: because each is ungraspable, beginningless, endless, they allow me to start from them and return to them again and again. They remind me that I learn the most when I know the least; that whenever I feel virtuous I stumble over my self-righteousness; that doubt leads to clarity, beauty forms from the play of discord and resolution, and difficulty leads to ease when I can let my clumsiness give way to good-natured laughter.

Zen and Taoism are allergic to preaching but addicted to paradox. Teachers and their sermons are seasoned with a mixture of the umami of respect and the salt of iconoclasm. When we give a Dharma talk, we often say we are making a mistake on purpose: we apologize for being misleading and ask our listeners to wash out our words from their ears with soap.

I once heard someone ask my Zen teacher, Sojun Mel Weitsman, "You read about people who devote themselves to study with a single teacher for twenty or thirty years. You also read about people who are pilgrims traveling from teacher to teacher to learn from as many people as possible. Which do you think I should do?"

Mel thought for a while, then replied:

"All told, probably better to stick to the poison that you have."

42

The Tao gives birth to one,
one gives birth to two,
two gives birth to three,
three gives birth to ten thousand things:
ten thousand things with yin at their backs,
yang in their embrace,
breath blending both,
qi harmonious.
What the world hates most:
to be orphaned, insignificant, poor, and unworthy.
Yet kings and queens take these labels?
Some gain by losing,
some lose by gaining.
What others teach, so do I:
"Strong violent tyrants
do not die natural deaths."
Let this be my teacher.

WE LIKE TO SAY life is one thing after another, but things don't add up: they multiply. The universe begins with a timeless, dimensionless singularity, gives explosive birth to matter and energy, and the cosmic dust spirals in on itself and forms millions upon millions of stars.

A friend invites you to a party. You decide to bring a gift, drive to the store, and stop to fill up the car with gas while grabbing a snack at the station's convenience store. Counter cashiers and oil rig workers are now members of your party: the air has more carbon dioxide, the earth fewer fossils. You arrive at the shopping center and purchase something that reaches to the hands of factory workers in China.

It's nice, if you're feeling insignificant, to know that when you throw even a pebble into a pond the ripples spread out in circles that widen even as they weaken. The flip side of this, though, is that every action you take entangles your life with everything you touch. Perhaps the party you have been invited to conflicts with another friend's invitation (will someone's feelings be hurt?) or interrupts a home repair project (can the dripping faucet wait?). Perhaps at the party you will meet someone and fall in love; the next thing you know you're having children and worrying about earning enough money to pay for their education.

This is the stuff of our lives, full of grief and joy. There is plenty of room for both so long as they are balanced. Bright activity (yang) needs dark quiet (yin). But we are reluctant to pass up opportunities that promise rewards of enjoyment or promotion, and we are reluctant to let go of anything we are already committed to. So we act, and act, and act again, and the accumulation is not linear but exponential. The world's population is six times larger than it was just two hundred years ago.

Everyone wants peace, but not everyone can tolerate being peaceful. The lure of stimulation, especially in a society that believes more is better, can be exhausting. People speed to their yoga sessions and hope squeezing in a class on meditation will keep them calm during the day as they multi-task. We learn a relaxation technique that takes only a minute to perform: we then get so busy we forget to use it.

It is easy to fall into the tyranny of doing. The feeling that you should do more is a tyrant worse than any dictator. It will wear you out and bring not just an early demise but the daily death of a thousand stressful cuts. If you do not free yourself from this tyranny you'll die early, or daily, or both.

This is not just "stress." As Thomas Merton, the great Catholic priest, author, and mystic, wrote:

> To allow oneself to be carried away by a multitude
>   of conflicting concerns;
> to surrender to too many demands;
> to commit oneself to too many projects;
> to want to help everyone in everything—
>   *is to succumb to violence.*

Doing too much is doing violence to your life. It doesn't matter if you do too much from a selfless intention to do good, from greed for advancement, fear of external consequences, or a guilty feeling you're not offering enough to the people you love. If you don't make room to stop and fully appreciate each moment, you'll miss your life as it rushes by.

———

Children love to hear the same story over and over again. One night I was putting my daughter to bed and she asked me to read her favorite bedtime story, Roald Dahl's *The BFG*, about a Big Friendly Giant who brings dreams to children, for what seemed to be the three-hundredth time.

I didn't want to. I was feeling pressured by a long list of to-dos I had to accomplish before I could relax and retire to bed myself. I picked up the book somewhat grudgingly and began reading to her more rapidly than usual, hoping she'd fall asleep so I could get on to my errands.

My daughter interrupted me: "No, Daddy, do the special voice you use for the BFG."

I paused, irritated. Wasn't it enough that I was reading to her what she wanted? Did I have to expend the energy and take the time to act out the characters too?

I looked at her and was struck by her joy, eagerness, and love. I thought of how short a time she would be a child open to this kind of intimacy. I realized if I just went through the motions of reading, I would regret the missed opportunity once she had grown older. So I gave up on accomplishing anything more that night, took a deep breath, and began the story over again.

The BFG visited both my daughter and I that night. Just as in the story, the Big Friendly Giant blew beautiful dreams through our window into our waking sleep.

43

The softest, most pliable thing in the world
overrides the hardest of all things in the world.
That which is not
penetrates though there's not the slightest crevice or crack.
Wonderful, wonderful,
effortless effort!
Wordless teaching:
returning to silence,
thinking nonthinking.
Beneficial nondoing,
rare realization,
incomparable, matchless.

PEACE IS IN EVERY STEP, as Thich Nhat Hanh says—but it relies on the ground underneath our feet.

Walking through a woodland, the forest floor yields to our weight. Because it yields, it can absorb the impact. Hiking, you enjoy the pleasure of a good tread beneath your feet; your stride transfers energy to the earth, which in turn absorbs the momentum and gives it back to you in a mild rebound, propelling you forward.

It is hard to feel a spring in your step when you are pounding a pavement or sitting in an automobile. We build our highways to be smooth and unyielding but they crack under the strain of use and the vagaries of natural weathering. Hard invokes hard: our manufactured infrastructure requires more work from us to maintain than do self-sustaining natural ecosystems. To the extent your bones and blood vessels are rigid, they are more likely to fracture under shocking impacts; supple minds are less susceptible to breakdowns in the face of stress.

Perhaps the hardest of all things in the world is our mind's tendency to lock us into dualistic thinking. Dualism polarizes us into mutually opposing concepts: hard/soft, is/isn't, good/bad, effort/sloth. In our increasingly digital society this seems natural, but the real world is analog not digital: there are degrees of ease as well as hurt, and neither excludes the other.

Anyone who has had to deal with chronic pain knows the more you fight it, the worse it gets. When you stop trying to harden yourself against it and instead let it flow through you, it is easier to bear. There are many ways to do this: you can soften around its edges, opening to the relief that comes with more space. You can focus on a different part of the body that is unaffected by agony (earlobes and toes are often good spots); you can even plunge into the center of the pain and find an empty pivot point.

If you think you can only escape suffering by avoiding pain, you will never liberate yourself from distress. If you think you can only feel peaceful when you are not upset, you will never experience equanimity. If you think you can only meditate in the absence of thought, you will never experience mental clarity. If you believe you only realize yourself through your achievements, you may feel inadequate when you are not accomplishing something.

Stop making yourself. Stop making excuses, stop making images, stop making comparisons, until you can stop stopping.

How do you stop stopping? The key is enjoying yourself, appreciating all experiences without separating them into good or bad. Then you are able to engage fully in whatever you are doing without worrying about the outcome, and your undivided activity is an effortless effort. This is doing nondoing, a field in which, whether you are quiet

or active, your divisions shatter into so many motes and all that is left
is sparkle: your practice is wonderfully continuous and you are realized
through and through.

———

When I was in college I had a friend who, like me, had been learning
yoga. He was more experienced than I was.

On one occasion I mentioned that I hadn't had time to practice yoga
that day and I felt guilty about it.

He turned to me with some surprise and said:

"Gee, on days when I don't get a chance to practice yoga, I don't feel
guilty—I just miss it."

44

Your reputation or your body:
which is more dear?
Your body or your possessions:
which is more precious?
Your losses and your gains:
which is more harmful?
Loving excessively
the cost is high.
Hoarding treasures
the losses are heavy.
Content with enough
you don't suffer disgrace.
Knowing when to stop
you're preserved from all peril.
This Way
is long-lasting.

EVERY EITHER/OR is a misleading question.

In the nineteenth century if you asked a gentleman whether his honor or his life were more dear, he would quickly answer "honor." Today, when reputations rise and fall with internet cycles, few people would be willing to die to preserve their good name. Both views, though, are one-sided; in fact the body of your reputation depends on both your living and how you live, and these in turn depend on how you're willing to die.

The logical disjunction of either/or can lead to false choices, allowing us to only see the differences that divide us when in reality our lives are fields wide enough to encompass opposites as well as everything in between. We are accustomed to the Aristotelian logic of the excluded middle: once you have "A," you cannot simultaneously have "not-A." If something is black, it is not white. Of course we recognize there are shades of grey, compounds of experience, and mixtures of feelings, but when two states are diametrically opposed we think you cannot both be and not-be the same state at the same time.

We're wrong, misled by a binary logic that's helpful for problem solving but overly restrictive for dealing with our actual experience in an indeterminate world. Light "cannot" be both wave and particle, but it is. We think we "shouldn't" ever hate someone we love, but we do. We can admire and resent, be angry and understanding, scared and brave all at the same time.

Centuries ago the great Buddhist sage Nagarjuna developed a form of logic that transcends either/or by embracing a full range of simultaneous existences: every thing is at once A, not-A, both A and not-A, and neither A nor not-A. This may sound unremarkable in the abstract, but its consequences are profound. It means all being is simultaneously alive, dead, both alive and dead, and also neither alive nor dead.

Nagarjuna's schema is based on Buddha's realization of the necessary unity of form and emptiness: things exist but without any fixed essence, and emptiness itself has no fixed characteristic. This logic can be difficult to comprehend; as Chuang Tzu points out, it's easy to think of something being present or absent but difficult to grasp the absence of absence. When you divide anything by zero you are in unknown territory; divide zero by zero and all bets are off.

We are used to seeing the world as a place where gain and loss are mutually exclusive. We rejoice at the birth and grieve at the death of a child. This is natural, but incomplete. Life and death are not opposites, but partners; each depends on the other. At this moment, if many of the cells in your body were not dying, there'd be no room for new cells to arise. Birth adds burdens and death offers release; in the midst of our happiness at a child's birth we may feel anxious about our ability to care for it and jealous of the attention a baby siphons from our spouse; if a child dies after a long illness we may feel guilt at the relief that comes from no longer having to take her to medical appointments and watch her suffer.

Mourning is natural; so, too, is the resurrection of joy. Love and grief are as inseparable as birth and death. This does not mean one should not love but that, if you are to be happy in love, you must not count the cost.

When loving, never ask "is it worth it?" Only so long as love is worthless will it be free to revive you. When you begin to evaluate and enumerate love, it becomes never enough.

Loving excessively, grasping at what you love and feeling however much love you receive (or give) is insufficient, will turn love to grief. Jealousy will drive your lover away; you will perceive your only child's leaving home as a loss rather than a blossoming, and the more you love life the more you will fear death.

Our being is rich with possibilities. When "either/or" expands so we can feel "both, and," then every event of our lives expands our horizons. Life and death, love and loss, body and mind form a harmonious whole. Because being itself is beyond gain and loss, it is always enough.

———

A good friend of mine, Jennie Yee, came down with cancer shortly after we both completed graduate school. She fought the cancer off, married, had a child and a fruitful career during which she contributed a great deal to her community. Unfortunately, when her daughter was around ten years old, Jennie's cancer returned and she died.

At her funeral, people said her life was too short. I thought of how her life could have ended a decade earlier, and how rich her life had been over the years she had been given. I felt sad for her daughter, but I also felt that—like my friend Joel, who I mentioned earlier—Jennie's life was complete as it was.

We can yearn for more: that my mother who died at seventy could have lived until seventy-one to see her second granddaughter walk or eighty-seven to see her graduate high school; that my friend Jennie could have had another eight years to help her child through adolescence. A person can die at a young age or an old age, but a person's life span is neither long nor short: it is an arc that, spanning birth to death, is complete in itself and comprises part of a much larger circle.

It reminds me of what one of my aunts has written on her tombstone. She had been a travel agent in the days of all-inclusive one-price-fits-all tours and often had to handle customers who wanted a discount by skipping a hotel in one city or a meal in another. She had to tell them if they wanted to take the tour, they couldn't pick and choose. If you go to her burial site, you'll see this inscription on her gravestone:

"Life is a package deal."

45

Great perfection seems lacking;
rely on it, though, to never wear out.
Great fullness seems empty;
rely on it, though, to never run dry.
Great straightness appears crooked.
Great skill appears crude.
Great eloquence appears inarticulate.
Activity overcomes cold;
stillness overcomes heat.
Tranquil and clear
the world finds itself
putting itself
right as *It is.*

LEARNING TO LIVE with your flaws is how you perfect yourself.

I tend to be a little suspicious of spiritual teachers who present themselves as fully enlightened gurus who have found the one-size-fits-all secret to happiness. I'm uneasy when psychotherapists insist research shows their technique is the only empirically validated path to psychological health. I'm much more inclined to listen to those who are forthright about all the ways they are lacking: how they learn from stumbling and falling short.

Every time a great musician plays a piece he experiences something that leads to playing it the next time with a slightly different phrasing or a more subtle coloring. Every time a great athlete has a superlative performance she learns more about coordination and timing so that her future efforts will shave a fraction of a second off her time or obtain a millimeter more of height. But this kind of search for perfection does not eliminate our need to include our errors in our efforts.

Musicians who aim only for perfection can end up, like Glen Gould, retreating from the messiness of live performance into the sterility of a recording studio, doing take after take but never feeling content. In contrast, the great classical pianist Vladimir Horowitz often made mistakes, but although he'd hit wrong notes in performances he was able to reach heights of expressiveness that transcended technique.

Athletes who cannot tolerate their mistakes after an error can let self-blame and self-scrutiny propel them into a slump. In the moral realm, someone who adheres rigidly to a set of absolute moral rules often comes across as shallow and brittle. Not surprisingly, those who grip most desperately to black-and-white moral absolutes are often those whose lives shatter when their faults lead to earthquakes of transgression.

Living is an art that calls for continuous practice, going straight ahead along a crooked path. Portia Nelson's "Autobiography in Five Short Chapters" tells the story of a person who walks down a street, falls into a hole in the sidewalk, denies it's her fault, feels hopeless, and takes forever to find a way out. Subsequently she walks down the same street pretending not to see the hole and falls in; walks down the street with her eyes open, falls in, acknowledges her fault, and gets out quickly; walks down the same street but walks around the hole. Finally, the autobiography ends with her walking down another street.

The new street will also have a new hole.

Continuous practice has no set goal, no fixed end-point. Continous practice does not promise to free us of all our problems, nor does continuous practice insist we self-flagellate so we can reach a pinnacle of purity. Continuous practice is a circle dance. Fortunately, when we have the opportunity to focus on practicing over and over with a form of life we've fallen in love with, the closer we come to the heart of the form the more we appreciate its depths are inexhaustible; we revel in the impossibility of ever reaching a point where we could completely master it, we feel gratitude that there is no ending point.

Wouldn't it be awful if there were some ultimate performance of a musical piece or an athletic feat? It would mean there would be nothing left to explore. Wouldn't it be terrible if we could read the mind of our lover and never have any further discoveries to delight us?

The more you love, the more you realize how utterly impossible it is to fully close the gap between you and the person you love. The more you realize how wonderful it is to simply be alive as yourself, the more you experience the gap between your limitations and your possibilities. Shunryu Suzuki liked to say: "each of you already is, was, and will be perfect . . . and you could use a little improvement."

It is this very gap that engenders the creative tension of form and formlessness, emptiness and fulfillment. Somehow, this jagged world awry keeps finding itself in equilibrium. Somehow, when our flawed self feels it cannot go on, we fall asleep and wake up in the morning and continue on our way.

At each moment, everything in the world finds itself right where it is. So do you.

———

When I was a young man in Japan learning shakuhachi (the Japanese bamboo flute), my teacher invited me to attend a concert featuring a rare performance by his father, who had been his teacher. He was then about eighty years old. I was excited to hear my master's master but crestfallen during the concert; his tone was wobbly and weak, his phrasing short and breathy.

After the concert my teacher asked me what I thought. I mumbled something polite about the privilege of hearing his father. My teacher laughed and said:

"You didn't think much of his performance, did you? That's because you expected him to sound like me or some other forty-year-old. What you don't realize is he sounded like an eighty-year-old—*exactly* like an eighty-year-old should sound!"

46

When the world practices Tao
the finest racing steeds are used to provide manure for the fields;
when the world does not practice Tao
war horses are raised on the border.
No vice is more onerous than being ruled by desire.
No calamity is more disastrous than insatiable greed.
No curse is worse than grasping at more.
The contentment that comes from knowing enough is enough
is abiding contentment in truth.

Too OFTEN we run around trying to satisfy ourselves without really knowing what will suffice. People race to line up overnight at stores holding a special sale; sometimes they trample each other competing for the limited supply of prize items.

Competitions can be fun. They can create mutual respect in participants, spurring each to exercise her very best abilities. However, when competition is contaminated by desire and greed, love of the game is replaced by love of self-aggrandizement. Then rivalries lead not to revelry but to war.

Capitalists proclaim their system "won" the twentieth century's Cold War and say this proves that competition is the best way to organize society. Socialists and the counterculture sometimes insist competition is inherently evil, forgetting that when we point to evil we create an enemy, and when we meet an enemy we always find ourselves staring back at us.

Cooperation and competition each fail when enshrined alone. Too much cooperation, and you will have the burlesque of two people at a doorway, each motioning the other to go first. Too much competition, and whoever grabs first place through the door may suffer a knife in his back from the hand of his rival.

What if the doorway is a gateless gate, one so wide we are all in it together? This is the fragile blue earth as seen from the moon. Seeing it, we are reminded our resources are limited. We have a choice: we can fight over them, or we can find the best ways to cooperate so that enough will be enough.

Greed holds no friendship for enough but always grasps for more. Greed seduces us into thinking we can *be* more by *getting* more; greed even sets up subtle contests within ourselves, pitting the next thing we will acquire against what we have, competing to see which will win the prize and provide contentment.

It is easy to fall into the trap of thinking if we only had a little more money, or a little more time, or a little more love, we would feel content. This defers to the future what is better experienced immediately. If you stop looking ahead, slow down, and pay attention to whatever is right in front of you, you'll often find you have enough to satisfy you.

Contentment is not dependent on clutching a quantity but on the way you caress the qualities of your life. The last time you felt contentment, was it because you had a great deal of something you desired, or because you were in a warm embrace that was mutual, neither too tight nor too loose?

———

A little while ago I noticed that during meals I had a habit, while I was still chewing one bite of food, of using my fork to gather the next mouthful. I decided to put down my fork and not pick it up again until after I had swallowed what was already in my mouth. I find when I do this my enjoyment increases; as I'm more aware of what I'm eating, I'm better able to savor the flavor of each forkful. I'm then more easily contented and find I need to eat less to feel satisfied—though sometimes I'll have an extra taste or two for the sheer pleasure of it. Eihei Dogen described it:

> There was his knowing what rice is after he had fully satisfied himself.
> And there was his being satisfied from having completely eaten the rice.
> And there was his full awareness of the rice satisfying him.
> And there was his having been fully satisfied and yet continuing to eat his rice.

Thirty years ago, traveling a back road on Cape Cod, I stumbled into a small general store where they made fresh, homemade donuts. They were the platonic ideal of donuts: warm, light, neither too oily nor too dry, crisp crusts coating the slightly sweet cakes. When I tried to revisit the store several years later, though, it had vanished. Ever since, I was on a quest to find another such donut. I'd go out of my way to places advertising fresh-made donuts, but each time I only found disappointment.

A little while ago, passing through high desert and pine forest on my way to Crater Lake, I passed a tiny general store which had a sign: "fresh donuts made daily." By this time I'd suffered enough donut disappointments and had nearly given up. But I wanted to stretch my legs so I parked and went in; the ten-year-old girl behind the counter handed me a just-made round marvel. One bite confirmed this was IT, donut heaven: I'd found the Grail. After savoring and devouring the donut, I prepared to order some more. They cost just three for a dollar. BUT . . .

I was surprised to realize I didn't want three more donuts. I'd eaten a large breakfast a little while ago, and right then I couldn't stomach even one more donut. I *wanted* to want more, but I could tell that since I wasn't hungry, eating another donut wouldn't be as satisfying as the first one. I thought of buying some and bringing them with me, but I knew they really needed to be eaten immediately and wouldn't be as good if I ate them a few hours later.

I felt sad. After thirty years' search I'd found the Ultimate Donut but could only eat one. I doubted I'd ever come back this way again, and to have just one donut after so long a search didn't seem right.

I was happy I was able to be sufficiently satisfied that I didn't overstuff myself. Yet I couldn't help but ask, "Is this, then, all there is to the end of a quest? Just ONE donut?" I even felt some regret the quest had been fulfilled. Perhaps I needed a new quest.

Do you happen to know any place that makes a really good banana cream pie?

47

Without going out your door,
you can know the whole world.
Without peering through your window,
you can see the Way of Heaven.
The farther people go
the less they know.
Therefore the sage knows without going,
sees without looking,
and completes without doing a thing.

GLOBALIZATION REMINDS US we're all interconnected, but it also distracts us with hazy, sometimes romanticized visions of exotic locales far away. Seeking the truth of yourself in a distant place or time can lead you to miss the whole world fully present in every instant at every place. Poets remind us that if you know how to look, you can see the universe in a grain of sand.

We can stumble by too much looking ahead with anticipation and too much looking back with regret, while our current lives are so full it is easy to get lost and lose track of what is most dear to us. In the busy necessities of commuting to work, answering phone calls, responding to emails, and making sure the children do their homework, we can get so stressed out we may fantasize about escaping to some other place or time, and forget to enjoy what we are doing.

When we seek outside and far away from ourselves it is an unintentional self-imposed blindness, like looking for the glasses perched on your forehead. When our eyes only focus on some narrow self-centered point, our depth of field is too shallow to sustain us. When our eyes soften—perhaps half open or half closed—and we allow our inner eye room to roam, we have access to dimensions that stretch unbroken within, without, and all around.

Physicists know the dimensions of our existence are mysterious. Newton was fully aware he'd left "space" as an undefined given; Einstein intertwined space with time but couldn't anticipate the quarkiness of subatomic uncertainties. Modern physicists searching for unified theories confess they do not fully understand either space or time. Zen Master Dogen, though, teaches us that the self is time and that space is finding yourself where you are.

When I was in college, the title of a book by Ram Dass became a popular saying: "Be Here Now." That saying is not quite correct, though: it sounds like a commandment to force yourself into the present. The fact is, you are always present, because here is now.

If the bottom-line question is "Who am I?" ultimately, the answer has to be "Here I am."

If you ask, "what is 'here'?" ultimately you must answer, "Now."

You, I, and everything are the expression of here-and-now. Being time, you are every moment complete. You are here, and here is you.

———

I was born in 1950 and grew up in a Jewish family still reeling from the Holocaust of World War II. Holding fast to being a Jew was drummed into me, yet there were dark undercurrents of fear, guilt, and anger. I felt confused by my parents' passionate insistence on maintaining a Jewish identity coupled with their lack of any regular religious practice except on Passover and the High Holidays. I found little sense of spirituality in the religious instruction I received at my temple; it seemed to rely a great deal on shame to enforce compliance to its tenets, and the pride at being Jewish also felt as if it contained subtle strains of anger and contempt for non-Jews. In fact, I started to feel depressed whenever I entered a Jewish temple.

When I reached college I was unclear about my personal identity and started looking for guidance in spiritual traditions far from my own. So I was somewhat surprised when I attended my first Zen meditation retreat in college and heard the teacher, Joshu Sasaki Roshi, say that if we were Jewish or Christian (or any other faith) we would need to become good Jews or Christians before we could become good Zen students. This led me to Martin Buber's *Tales of the Hasidim*, and I encountered the following:

> Reb Zusia of Anipoli used to say:
> "When the day comes that I must account for my life before the Heavenly Tribunal, they will not ask me: 'Zusia, why weren't you Moses?'
> I fear they will ask me a more difficult question: 'Zusia, why weren't you Zusia?' And to that it will be more difficult to answer."

This story, coming from my own tradition, mirroring my own conflicts, resonated to my marrow. I needed to wander before reconciling with my Judaism, but through zazen I was able to let go of the husks of my tradition and return to its heart and to myself.

There is a Zen koan:

> A monk named Hui Ch'ao says to Fa Yen, "Hui Ch'ao asks the teacher, what is Buddha?"
> Fa Yen replies, "You are Hui Ch'ao."

When I encountered this koan I remembered Reb Zusia and was reminded to come back to myself.

48

Seek learning: increase daily.
Practice the Way: decrease daily.
Lose and let go and decrease
until you reach nondoing.
Nondoing, yet nothing is left undone.
To rule the world,
don't interfere with its going about its business.
If you are a busybody,
you can't rule the world.

WHEN LEARNING is only concerned with acquiring useful knowledge it becomes conflated with power and control. Corporations seek an accumulation of patents to gain a competitive advantage; governments seek the sequestration of secrets to gain increased control over their people and neighboring nations.

We sometimes accumulate knowledge to use as a source of pride, displaying what we have learned as badges of identity. Memorizing the stats of your local sports team lets others know "I'm a fan"; studying the basics of basidiomycetes informs others "I'm a biology professor with a specialty in mushrooms." To the extent we do this, our information is transformed into effigies of ourselves. When we inflate ourselves with expertise, ballooning egos can be easily punctured; threatened with deflation, interactions with others can become prickly.

When we are full of ideas we filter our experience; we become susceptible to confirmation bias (focusing on information that confirms our preconceptions) and disconfirmation bias (being skeptical about information that contradicts our prior beliefs). The more we are attached to what we've learned, the more prone we are to the Semmelweis Reflex: the tendency, if the facts don't fit your preexisting theory, to throw out the facts.

Our knowledge is also vulnerable to the law of unintended consequences. Alfred Nobel invented dynamite to help make nitroglycerine safer for use in construction work but saw TNT turned to terror's use. Discovering the secrets of the atom made possible not just transistor radios but also nuclear bombs. Physicians have so much expertise they often are quick to intervene but the medications and procedures they administer can result in side effects that interfere with the body's ability to go about its business of healing itself.

Our minds are sometimes so crowded with the learning we have taken in that we cannot think straight. Ideas can be pernicious; sayings can stick in our minds as stubbornly as advertising jingles. A little girl who hears a mother say "from too much laughing comes crying" may absorb a message she should not enjoy herself too much; a little boy who spills his milk and hears his teacher scold "clumsy!" may feel increasingly inept.

Of course learning can be beneficial as well as injurious; it helps us adapt to changing circumstances, and to the extent that learning teaches us how much we do not know, it can be a source of humility and wonder. We are curious beings who love even useless information; learning for its own sake can be a joy. Nonetheless, there are dangers even here. When we acquire knowledge we lose some of the innocence of direct perception; the moon may be a little less romantic for lovers now that people have walked on its surface and beamed back photos of cold dust and barren craters. Furthermore, if you stuff your brain too full with facts you may have trouble sorting trivia from truth.

Suzuki Roshi used to say, "in the beginner's mind there are many possibilities; in the expert's mind there are few." If we want to widen our field of possibilities, we need to let go, and let go, and let go again. When we know the not-knowing of beginner's mind we can find unimagined facets in even the most familiar encounters: instead of taking our love of many years for granted, each morning we can discover her anew.

When we empty ourselves out, we clear the slate to become more receptive. Be careful, though: when you drop your filters and let go of preconceptions, you can find yourself face to face with reality itself.

———

A busybody has difficulties self-adjusting. Where there is an excess of control, it is hard to relax.

Through studying yoga, I learned how to control my breathing. I applied this to Rinzai Zen breath counting, focusing intensely on deep breaths to cleanse myself of discriminative thought and strengthen my *hara* (the seat of spiritual and physical energy, located in the lower abdomen). I trained myself to be so intentional in my breathing that when I began Soto Zen meditation and was told to "just let the breath come naturally" I had a terrible time finding a way to breathe willingly instead of willfully. Often my breath felt too shallow or too rapid, but if I tried to resume controlled breathing, it now felt forced.

I developed back pain. Hoping to alleviate it, I began practicing Dayan ("Wild Goose") Qigong. Most qigongs emphasize breathing exercises but Dayan lets the breath come naturally, without interference from thinking about it too much. (Apparently because of this, it has helped many of my patients with lung problems who had troubles with effortful breathing).

Initially I approached qigong as a way to increase my control over my body, and I had difficulties understanding when my teacher, correcting me, would exhort me to be "just natural." I struggled to learn what seemed to be strange and even unnatural movements; I didn't realize they only seemed this way to me because I was trying to acquire them as a set of skills I could add to my spiritual resume. I had to learn to stop interfering and let the flow of *qi* go about its business.

Gradually, practicing the same set of movements over and over, they became so familiar I started to let go, do less, and trust my body and mind to self-adjust. I began to stop "doing" the movements and allow them to "just move."

Through this practice I began to learn to stop "doing" *shikantaza* meditation and "just sit." Shunryu Suzuki advises us it is a mistake to think "I" am doing meditation. I began to offer myself instruction: "let the meditation do the meditating . . . let the qigong do the qigong."

Body, breath, and mind began to have room to cooperate with each other naturally. It became possible to stop "breathing" and just breathe. As zazen and qigong stopped being a matter of learning to do some special practice, they became gateways to great ease and joy.

49

The sage has no set mind but simply is
the ordinary mind of all people.
To the good she is good,
to the not good she is also good.
This is the goodness of nature.
To those who are true he is true;
to those who are untrue he is also true.
This is the truth of nature.
As for the sage's presence in the world:
one with *It,* mind's auspicious merging.
People strain to focus their ears and eyes;
sages have a gentle smile for all.

IF YOUR MIND IS SET, it is limited.

Every time a neuron fires in your brain it becomes a little easier for it to fire again. With enough repetition, your habits become smooth grooves. This is fine; it would take a lot of energy to have to decide each time you tie your shoes which lace goes where. If, however, your grooves become ruts, they will confine you to an eroding gully.

When your mind is less set, it adapts more easily to changing conditions. Although our brains are most plastic when we are young, brain plasticity does not disappear when we age. We can reorganize ourselves in response to novel experiences, and even when upset by a head injury or derailed by a stroke, our brain redistributes its operations and finds new channels for its functions.

The mind is not confined to the brain, or even to thoughts, conscious or otherwise. Mind has its own being: it flows over and around obstacles, down toward the ocean, finding peace even in its froth. Ordinary mind, like water, likes being level; it is attuned to equanimity.

People often mistake equanimity for being constantly calm to the point of being immune to the ups and downs of life, but equanimity simply means "treating everything as equal." Our open "unset" mind is exquisitely sensitive and registers whatever comes, but it does so as a clear mirror, reflecting whatever it encounters without discriminating whether it is pretty or ugly, good or bad. Mind is true to itself and all around it.

Ordinary mind is common as the ground and unspectacular, more stable than any brilliant fireworks or flashy constructions. Mind is the space within which thoughts arise and fall, the field where perceptions bubble up and burst, the silence that has room for every kind of feeling. Thoughts, perceptions, and feelings come and go, but the ground of ordinary mind is always present. A hurricane may blow through; there may be rainbows or clear sunshine. The mind receives them all the same, true to its nature and to all it meets.

When we meditate in the shikantaza practice of Soto Zen, we return to ordinary mind. We do not try to stop thoughts or feelings or perceptions; we do not try to control them but we also do not let them control us. We just make room for everything. People are sometimes disappointed that this meditation does not have esoteric techniques to foster ecstatic mental states or enlightenment experiences. If you have some kind of enlightenment experience and tell a Soto Zen teacher about it, she is likely to reply, "That's nice. What now?" It can be a little deflating to the ego to not have anything special to cling to.

Chuang Tzu says, "If a man follows the mind given him and makes it his teacher, then who can be without a teacher? To insist upon your rights and wrongs is like saying that you set off for Yueh today and got there yesterday." When you let go of self-centered views and stop worrying about your rights and your wrongs, your set views of good and bad, everything and everyone becomes a teacher re-minding you of your true self. Then you can respond to all with a clear heart and a gentle smile.

What have you learned from your teacher today?

———

Shortly before completing a Fulbright teaching at the National Institute of Mental Health and Neuroscience (NIMHANS) in India, I heard my friend Kiran Rao say, "Whenever I have some difficulty, I ask myself: What can I learn from this?" I liked this, so I resolved to apply it. I anticipated it would be helpful for extraordinary, dramatic lessons. I didn't understand it would be most important to practice it in the ordinary frustrations of everyday life.

The next morning I had to mail some packages from the post office. Knowing the India of 1988 was still buried in red tape and bureaucracy I'd reserved the whole day for the task. I went to the post office first thing in the morning so I'd be done in time for my farewell party at NIMHANS at six that evening. By 3:00 p.m. I'd gotten through the queues, obtained the necessary documents and stamps. Just one more step remained: to take my four boxes down to the basement where they would be sewn into the burlap bags the post office required before affixing seals and sending them off. Plenty of time to get to NIM-HANS by 6:00 p.m.

The very elderly attendant in the dimly lit basement was in no hurry. He looked at his needle; looked at his thread; picked up the needle; picked up the thread; moved the needle to eye level; moved the thread up . . . it took him ten minutes to thread the needle. He then put the needle on the bag; looked up; let go of the needle with one hand; put his other hand on the needle; slowly pulled it through and extended the thread to its full eighteen inches. Then he put the needle down, licked his fingers, licked the thread, and began all over again. It took him thirty minutes to do ten stitches and finish one bag.

At this pace I knew I would be late for my farewell party, but the phones weren't working and I couldn't call to let the people at NIM-HANS know. As the needle and thread continued their journey slow stitch by slow stitch, and the minutes passed and I became later and later, my anxiety and frustration built. I kept asking myself, "What can I learn from *this*?"

I arrived an hour late to my own party. I started to apologize but the head of the department stopped me, saying: "Actually, I'm glad you were late. The faculty here never really gets a chance to spend time with each other. It's been wonderful to have this unexpected amount of time to chat together—we've been enjoying ourselves immensely."

50

People appear in birth-and-death.
Three out of ten are partners of life;
three out of ten are partners of death;
and three out of ten, in living, move toward the execution ground
because they grasp at life, seeing it only as *LIFE*.
I have heard
those who know how to nourish true life
travel the hills, fearless of wild ox and tigers,
enter battles without armor or shields;
wild ox find no place to sink their horns,
tigers find no place to sink their claws,
weapons find no place to sink their blades.
And why?
Because there is no place for death to enter in.

MOST OF US don't really believe we will die. We know we'll die in the same way we know the sun will some day burn out: as a remote fact, not a personal experience.

In the past death was more familiar. Infant mortality and death in childbirth were common; both the elderly and the young usually died at home in the presence of their family. These days we sequester the dying in hospitals, nursing homes, and hospices; this makes death a greater unknown and more frightful.

Our consciousness rebels against the possibility of its passing. Much like children who fight falling asleep because they don't want to miss anything, we seek the stimulation of more experience. Often we feel the most alive when we live on the edge; many people—especially young adults, with their hunger for "LIFE"—seek out experiences that involve the risk of dying. Skydiving, surfing, ski jumping, racing cars: in these days when antibiotics and clean water have largely banished death to the old, and the unknown spaces on maps have been filled in by satellite photos, people need to work harder to find peril. This is one way we grasp at "LIFE."

Another way we grasp at "LIFE" is just the opposite: we try very hard to enhance safety as if by so doing we could outwit death. Parents don't let their children ride a bicycle without putting on a helmet; cars have seat belts and air bags; people go on diets and eat the latest foods to ensure they'll live on and on. It's almost as if we think people "shouldn't" die if they exercise, eat right, take proper precautions, and the doctors and alternative medicine gurus do their jobs.

All of this, of course, is to no avail. When death comes there is no escape, and the universe does not care much about our ideas of who deserves to die when from what. Fit long-distance runners keel over from sudden heart attacks; young children die from cancers usually seen in old age; innocent passersby are killed by a bullet meant for someone else; a routine medical procedure leads to complications and sudden death.

Some people are partners of death; they purposefully cultivate it. During the Romantic era it was almost *de rigeur* for any aspiring poet to die young. These days we have vampires and goths, self-cutters and autoerotic strangulations—not to mention the tens of thousands of deaths dealt each day in fantasy video games and television crime dramas.

Clutching at life and courting death both miss the point. Death and life just reflect different facets of the jewel of being. In a certain sense, life and death are illusions, mere labels we give to temporary states of being. Our physical substance is just a transient accumulation of quarks that combine, separate, come together, and fall apart; our consciousness is an accumulation of shifting quirks of perception: who knows what forms these may take prior to palpable parturition and subsequent to seeming cessation?

The great thing is to not be afraid of life, and to not be afraid of death. If you're afraid of living, you constrict yourself and the world shrinks. If you're afraid of dying, instead of being born afresh you become stale.

It's natural to experience fear; being yourself is inherently terrifying. Facing your fears takes courage, but because your being takes place in birth and death, because you cannot have one without the other, you need courage to be fully yourself.

Where can you find courage? Only in the place where you are. When you fully face a moment, you fully face yourself and become so engaged you forget yourself. Then there is no room to worry about life or death.

A few months ago, after crossing Tilman's pass in the Langtang Himalaya, my companion (a fellow Zen teacher) remarked to me that although she was scared when she looked up at the hanging glaciers abutting the pass, when she was actually traversing the icy expanse she was so absorbed she felt no fear. I replied that whenever I'm on a tricky section of trail, I do feel fear, but it is of the sort that heightens my alertness and, rather than leading me to worry about what will happen, instead helps me feel fully present.

Each of us was describing our experience of immediacy. When fully involved in the how of now, there is no other place, no other time. To paraphrase Eihei Dogen: life does not turn into death. Life is an expression complete this moment. Death does not turn into life. Death is an expression complete this moment. You don't call summer the end of spring, or autumn the beginning of winter. Each is fully itself every moment and simultaneously connected to everything that ever was and will be.

So are you. Just this, *just this*. As you read, there is nothing else but reading; here is your true life. As you close this book, kill it. Look up: here is true life, afresh.

—

One of my clients knew she was positive for the gene that causes Huntington's disease. People with this gene inevitably develop a dementia, usually between the ages of thirty-five and forty-four. There is no cure.

Four years earlier I had done a neuropsychological assessment for my client and she had been fine. This time, her assessment showed unmistakable signs the disease was beginning. I informed her of these results and said I was sorry. She asked me why I was sorry.

I was surprised at her response, since I knew she was fully aware of how the disease progressed and its implications of cognitive and physical degeneration. I told her I was sorry she had to face the symptoms she knew were now beginning.

She replied, "Don't feel sorry for me; I feel grateful. I find it so helpful to know I have little time left to me—so I live my life fully!

"I only feel sorry for other people who, not being aware how close they may be to illness and death, go through their days only half alive."

51

Tao gives birth to them,
rightness nurtures them,
matter forms them,
circumstances complete each one's uniqueness.
Thus all things honor Tao
and treasure Rightness
not because they are ordered to do so,
but because this is natural, spontaneous.
Tao begets the ten thousand things,
Rightness nurses them
steadies them trains them adjusts them
protects them ripens them buries them.
It gives birth without possessing,
cultivates without holding on,
guides without demanding control.
This is called deep mysterious Virtue.

EACH OF US is an expression of all that gave birth to us. We are beholden not just to our parents' gametes but also to the water that sustained their cells, the minerals and proteins that provided their structure, and the very sun that was the ultimate source of their energy. In a very real way, each of us is a child of the entire universe and nurtured by the same forces that guide its unfolding.

Laws of physics give form to our material substance; natural selection forms our species. Evolution ensures survival of the fittest, but "fittest" does not mean strongest or most dominant. Rather, those living beings that form the best match with the specific circumstances of their environment—those who find a good fit—thrive.

From our earliest years, everyone intuitively knows when something fits not too snugly nor too loosely, is not too hot nor too cold, but "just right." Finding the rightness of a good fit is a matter of mutual adjustments between the child and her environment. As a child you coached your parents how to satisfy your needs, but your family also insisted you fit in with them. The world's demands became more stringent as you got older; you were required to sit at a desk in a school and go out to recess when the clock struck ten. You were taught rules of what was right to want when, and when it was wrong to do what. This is inherent in all socialization, but being ordered around too much stifles spontaneity and creativity.

You can force things to fit, but forcing always involves a certain amount of violence. Forcing nature to fit human needs violates Rightness: irrigating a desert to bring forth green suburban lawns may look pretty but is another form of rape; the monoculture of using one hundred acres of land to produce nothing but tightly-packed roses is a violation of beauty. Requiring a restless child to sit still in a classroom is a mild, socially acceptable form of coercion, which doesn't fit the child very well but suits the needs of school systems trying to regulate large numbers of unruly children.

There are alternatives to forced fit. Compassionate cultivation assists nature to bring forth what is most fitting to each being. We can prune a tree to help it find the space it wants for its branches and fruit, and carve a piece of marble not to our specs but to reveal the shape of the David latent within it. We can mentor a child not to shape him to our desires but to help him find his true self and unique abilities; we can assist an adult woman to find her true face before she was born, the one uncorrupted by myths of beautiful princesses and ugly witches.

You need to find both what is fitting for you and how you fit into your life—how to be in accord with your circumstances in a way that rightly nurtures your unique self-expression. This does not need to be anything special. Embracing a lover, expressing sincere interest in a friend, admitting when you are bored are all ways of finding Rightness. There is virtue in simply being aware when discord arises and doing nothing beyond giving it room and time to develop until it's ripe to right itself.

Today, what felt "just right"? What nurtured this rightness in yourself and others? How about at this moment: is reading this book fostering your being? If not, put it down and come back to it only when and if it does.

———

When I train psychotherapists I strongly suggest they pay attention to a crucial but often neglected tool: their office chair. I've found my sitting posture during psychotherapy provides me with a sensitive barometer. Leaning forward or backward alerts me to my tendencies to be attached or averse to what a client is presenting; leaning left or right can tell me of my inclinations to be logical or sentimental, to do too much or too little. If the chair I use puts me in a position that collapses my chest I cannot breathe freely, while if the chair strains my lower back the spasms cause my mind to clench as well. Either impingement restricts my ability to listen to clients and meet them where they are.

When a chair is "just right," it nurtures you. It guides your posture and steadies your stature; it receives you but does not impose itself on you, leaving you free to come and go. This is the virtue of a good chair.

Mass-produced chairs have little virtue. In a movie theater, clinic waiting room, or workplace office with one hundred identical chairs and one hundred unique people, only one person's size and shape will find a chair that truly fits. Chairs without choices force us to fit them, rather than the other way around. If a chair is not aligned with the needs of your body, the chair trains your body to adapt to something that is not good for it. When a chair is not right for you, you may develop headaches, backaches, or other types of chronic pain. The effects can be subtle: you may feel tired, stale, "not quite right" with yourself or the world.

There are less obvious chairs in our lives. Everyone who nurtures in a way that truly fits and upholds without trying to possess has the virtue of a good chair. Teachers provide the seat of learning for their students, and the student responds by giving the teacher lessons on how to tutor; parents cradle the child cuddled on their lap, and the child responds naturally with love. Our minds can hold our bodies and our bodies support our minds without having to fight over who is the chairperson in charge.

Meditation cushions are usually round; they support us no matter what direction we face, allowing us to use them in any fashion we choose. They are very generous, so at our Zen center we bow to them before sitting down and bow again in gratitude as we get up.

52

The world has an origin:
the Great Mother.
Having reached the mother,
we know the child;
having known the child,
return and abide by the mother.
This is dropping body and mind
to find true safety.
Block the holes,
close the gates;
life is whole, without toil.
Open the holes,
meddle in affairs;
life leaks out, careworn.
Seeing the small is illuminated vision;
abiding in pliant softness is true strength.
Follow the streams of light back to return to their source,
look within for true vision
so you steer free of calamity.
Such is to follow
always-so, everlasting.

You not only can go home again, you must. The journey of being yourself is a process of always coming home. We all need to replenish the well-springs of our being by returning to our original dwelling place where we find true safety.

Our home is not a childhood fantasy, not a once-familiar house nor even people loved in a past time and remote place. Our true home is our origin, the source of our nurturance, the Great Mother; it includes Mother Earth who bears us as well as the biological mother who bore us. The Great Mother is always just so; the forms she takes are continuously changing, but although earth morphs into mountains and valleys and Mommy's features alter with age, each is eternally our mother.

Our society is still largely shaped by patriarchal habits. It emphasizes "onward and upward": go out, explore, conquer, get bigger. Our yearning to be cradled in our mother's embrace is seen as weakness, something to outgrow; we disparage stay-at-homes as "mama's boys" fearful to break free. Freedom, though, relies on the ability to both stay and leave, go in and out, to wisely view the experience of adulthood with the wondering eyes of a child.

If you are only parental and cannot exercise your natural need for play, if you cannot sometimes let go of your responsibilities and just enjoy yourself, you may become overly rigid; you risk disciplining your sons or daughters to the point where they become miniature parents to the child you deny within you. If you only amuse yourself, though, you may not develop the discipline necessary to go deeper in being yourself. It's fun to push your child on a swing; it's also a pleasure to be old enough to know how to swing on a swing yourself.

In extremis, in the hospital or on the battlefield, the strongest among us may call out for our mother. She may not be there physically, but her presence can still be felt. As a psychotherapist I often heard clients lament how their mothers had abused or abandoned them, and it is undeniable that some mothers (and fathers) itch to boil their children, swallow them up, or sell them to serve their own needs, drown them to purge them of sin. But every mother has given birth and at least for a moment put her skin next to her child's and exchanged the vital heat of being alive. Even though her hindrances may have been great and her delusions may have distorted the impulses of her good heart, resulting in harm and hurt, every mother has loved to whatever extent she was capable. In this way, every mother has passed some tendril of connection with the Great Mother on to each of her children.

Our actual mothers (and fathers), being only human, will sometimes fall short of what we feel we need, but the Great Mother greets all her children with equal love from the before prior to beginning, to the after subsequent to ending. Zen sometimes calls this Great Mother, this source of compassion and rest, "your original face before you were born." It is great beyond male or female, big or little, beyond even alive or dead; it cannot be constrained by such dualities.

When the world is too much with you and you are so filled with cares you cannot contain them, it can feel as if your life energies leak out. It is important at such times to be able to close the gaps, repair the breaks, and seal the holes to restore wholeness. To find the Great Mother you need only soften around your suffering. If only for a moment, block off the barrage of external stimulation that distracts you, close down your affairs in the world that drain and exhaust you. Look within: enfold yourself in the moving forms of stillness. Even in the dark nights of the soul, your Great Mother is always here.

A single breath, the smallest smile, is enough to provide the light for illuminated vision.

—

Nearly a quarter of a century has elapsed since my mother's death, but I still take comfort in her smile. My father used to say, "When Goldie smiles, the world lights up."

Like any human being she had her foibles and her fears, her disappointments and sometimes flares of fierce temper. But she was generous to everybody, a wonderful combination of soft-hearted and practical. Friends, family, distant relatives, even coworkers and casual acquaintances would, when faced with relationship problems, seek her out to get her advice; it was always compassionate but down-to-earth and sensible. She weathered the storms of my adolescence, tolerated my challenges, my sulks and fits of temper (though not without giving back as good as she got—she was no pushover).

Perhaps most important, she extended her love to anyone I loved and welcomed them to our family, whether or not they fit her ideas of who she'd like to see me with. She had compassion for anyone in difficulty regardless of the color of their skin or their politics or religion. In short, she embraced all that came to her. But when it came to protecting her family she could be fierce as a tiger.

Whenever we visited with our baby daughter Anna (her first granddaughter), her joy was boundless. One lovely summer day, my wife and I decided it would be nice to spend a little family time on the backyard grass outside.

My mother was many things, but she was not an outdoors person. She'd lived in an urban environment all her life. To her, anything green and growing was dangerous wilderness. So she took multiple precautions. She made sure Anna was wearing just the right clothes, not too warm but not too light. She tied a little bonnet to shade Anna's eyes. She swathed any exposed area of Anna's skin with sunscreen. She insisted my father mow and rake the lawn before we ventured forth. She got a blanket to put out on the grass: no, wait, that one would be too scratchy for the baby, use one of the nicer blankets. She cleaned the lawn furniture and resurrected an old beach umbrella to ward off too many ultraviolet rays.

Finally, everything was ready. We took the precious bundle of granddaughter outside, placed her on the blanket, and settled into the surrounding chairs.

We'd been sitting perhaps five minutes when my mother, ever alert to threats to her family's well-being, sat bolt upright. "*A bee!*" she cried, pointing to the winged menace. She immediately jumped up, swooped down to the baby and, shielding her defenseless granddaughter from the dreaded beast's stinger, scooped her up and rushed inside.

Okay, she was a little overprotective. Like every mother, she had her blind spots and limitations and bequeathed me mixed memories of appreciation and disappointment, fulfillment and loss. In gratitude, I bow to the Great Mother, the lovely, the holy, who gives light; in gratitude I bow also to my fleshly mother who gave me life.

53

If I have a little wisdom to follow the great Way,
it's only going astray that I'll fear.
The Great Path is very smooth and straight,
but people are fond of bypaths.
The courtyards are swept clean
but the fields are full of weeds
and the granaries empty.
They wear fancy clothes and carry sharp swords,
surfeited with food and drinks,
overflowing with possessions and wealth.
Thievery! Brazen bandits!
Holding more than they need——
this is not the Way.

IT'S EASY TO GO ASTRAY. We receive so many messages each day of what to think, how to eat, where to play, and when to sleep that we lose track of what smoothes our Way: we sacrifice our circadian rhythms to productivity and fill our consciousness with consumerism. Nature, though, gives it to us straight: the temperature of the earth, the currents of the oceans, and the composition of the air we breathe all tell us we are taking too much.

We tend to focus on what will immediately benefit us. Faced with forests, we see only the trees we can turn into lumber; we don't see how removing trees leads to mudslides that will inundate our homes. We build dams to hold back the force of water, build feedlots to efficiently enclose the grazing of the animals we feed on. We spray pesticides to hold back the encroachments of what we consider pests on "our" land; we think to hold back disease through prolific use of antibiotics. As a result of these efforts reservoirs silt up, salmon fail to spawn, methane chokes our air, cancers kill, and resistant strains of bacteria spring up.

In nature high flows to low, but man-made societies reverse this: those on the bottom are exploited to enrich those on the top. As I write this, the richest 1 percent of Americans account for 24 percent of the nation's income and hold 43 percent of its financial wealth. This is a remarkably skewed distribution, but it pales in comparison to the vast disequilibrium in global wealth: the three richest people in the world own assets that exceed the combined gross domestic products of the world's forty-eight poorest countries. These imbalances are unnatural departures from the Way.

We justify the imbalances we create with theories we concoct: trickle-down economics, social darwinism, and a general sense of entitlement that as humans we have a "right" to control nature (and each other). We even mistake the imbalances we've created as inevitable or normal: when most buildings have electricity, if a blackout interrupts the city's power supply the darkness of the night can seem an aberration. When most everyone around you eats three meals a day, it is difficult to really understand how a third of the world's population is underfed and another third is literally starving.

If we are aware of imbalances in our environment and society, as humans we may get angry at the injustices and shortsightedness we encounter. We are good at feeling self-righteous, anxious, or even ashamed at human malfeasance. The Way is not like this. Its rightness does not judge by human standards of fair and equitable; it doesn't get even but dispassionately redresses imbalances evenly.

When the dam bursts, it is impartial in drowning everyone in its path. When the antibiotic-resistant pandemic emerges, it infects rich and poor alike, without discriminating. When the wars and revolutions come to address the social inequities, violence topples the well-meaning along with the well-heeled.

———

One of my clients was from a famous, wealthy family. My client told me he was depressed because he was unemployed after failing at several business ventures. His brothers all had successful financial careers, but he had never really made a "go" of it and his failures filled him with shame and fear. In addition to not being very good at business he had never really enjoyed it. He enjoyed art and had some talent, but felt that he should not devote his time to it, that he needed a commercial career in order to measure up to others.

I explored the gravity of his worries about money, asking if he had any income coming in. He answered yes, he received an annual annuity of around $100,000. In addition his wife had always worked, enjoyed her job, and in fact they could manage on her salary alone. I knew he lived in an expensive area of town, so I inquired if he needed to obtain work in order to pay a hefty mortgage. He answered no, he had no mortgage, his house was all paid off. He was basically debt-free.

I asked him why he was so obsessed with finding employment that he did not really want or need. He had adequate income; his wife wasn't affected; his house was paid off: why not devote his time to being an artist, since he enjoyed that?

"If I don't get a job as an executive," he replied, "I'll have to resign from all my clubs."

Hearing this I felt a moment of surprise, and then a wave of sadness. How difficult to have so much and yet feel so trapped!

Having grown up in a family that, while not poor, struggled to scrape together enough money to get by, I have sometimes had to wrestle with feelings of anger and envy for people whose wealth gave them a smoother ride in the material world. Listening to this client, my conflicts in this area started to dissolve and give way to compassion at how a person can have so much more than he materially needs but still feel desperately deprived and fearful.

I have a roof over my head and enough to eat. Everything else I have beyond that is really more than I need, yet still I sometimes am envious of what my wealthier friends are able to enjoy. I feel better when I can summon sympathetic joy in their happiness. Sometimes, though, surrounded by surfeit, when I mistake my wants for my needs, it is easy to go astray.

54

What is well planted is not uprooted,
what is embraced fully does not slip away.
It is honored generation to generation without end.
Cultivating *this* in the self, Rightness becomes genuine;
Cultivating *this* in the family, Rightness becomes abundant;
Cultivating *this* in the community, Rightness endures;
Cultivating *this* in the nation, Rightness flourishes;
Cultivating *this* throughout the whole world, Rightness
    becomes universal.
Therefore study the self in the self,
study the family in the family,
study the community in the community,
study the nation in the nation,
and study the world in the world.
How do we know the world is really so?
Through *this*.

WHAT CAN YOU plant yourself in if not the soil of your self? Cultivating this self, though, is not the same as delving into your personal psychology.

You can get stuck in your ego's conflicts, your impulses' urges, your self-conscious praise and condemnation. These are a very small part of your true self. Psychotherapy can help your ego get "unstuck," but it runs the risk of misleading you into projects of self-improvement, of thinking self-knowledge comes from accumulating information about yourself. But your case history is not the story of your life, nor can it capture the electricity of current, lived events. Therapy works best when it frees you to expand your possibilities of experience in the present.

Your prior experiences—traumas and triumphs—can shape you, but they are not where you plant your true self. Your body and mind have a natural gravity that draws you to your center. It may not always be easy to find the routes to your roots: too often we think to find our origin in our past, that at bottom we are our befores. But roots do not only lead backward.

So long as you are growing, your roots are spreading deeper and wider. As you grow older you become aware of the depth of your generations of ancestors and the breadth of your living connections. Cultivating all that was, you tap into accumulations of wisdom; cultivating all that is, you realize you need never feel lonely.

The Zen teacher Eihei Dogen famously said, "To study Buddhism is to study the self; to study the self is to forget the self; to forget the self is to realize your self in each and all of the myriad things." Whether you call it Buddhism, the Way, God, or *just this*, you find your true self not in ideas about who you were or fantasies of who you might become but in being the simple things you do every day: how you hold a teacup, how you kiss your lover, how you interact with your family around the dinner table and the supper dishes, how you cooperate with the people you work with and how you work with the politicians who represent and misrepresent you in your nation and the world.

Cultivating the roots of *this* means becoming intimate with all the parts of ourselves within and without, our organs and our organizations. At that point we realize we are more than just people; we are a family, a community, a nation, and the world. Better put, the world is us.

We need to discover how to embrace not only our friends but all around us, including our supposed enemies, while still standing firm in the Way that accords with Rightness. This Rightness is not yours but everyone's. It is the concordance musicians find when they tune their instruments just so: the sound waves align with each other and the "beats" of interference coalesce.

When you tune yourself truly, you know it through your sense of being genuine, of being ordinary and whole. This is abundant Rightness beyond right or wrong, self or other.

Being natural is being universal. Start by being natural yourself.

———

In meditation practice people sometimes come up against disavowed, previously unknown parts of themselves. It can be painful to see the extent of one's egotism, anger, selfishness, narcissism, and greed.

One time I was feeling this way and, in some anguish and despair, asked my teacher, "How can I burn away this self?"

He replied, "Let the Self burn away the self."

55

One who fully embodies Rightness
can be compared with a newborn child.
Wasps and scorpions will not sting,
snakes and vipers will not bite,
fierce beasts will not attack,
raptors will not pounce.
The infant's bones are weak, sinews soft,
but its grip is firm.
As yet oblivious to sexual copulation,
not knowing male and female,
still its body is fully aroused.
Its life force perfect at its height,
it can scream all day yet never get hoarse
because it embodies harmony completely.
To know harmony is to know the always-so,
to know the always-so is to see clearly.
Trying to add more to life portends poorly;
controlling life's breath with your mind overstrains it.
Forcing things: excess vigor hastens decay.
This is not the Way.
What is not in accord with the Way
quickly crumbles.

YOU ARE A CORPOREAL BEING: you are literally some *body*. When your body and mind are in accord, you are undivided and whole.

Voluntary and involuntary nervous systems meet in the breath. If we don't think about our breath its rate adjusts to our activities; we can modify our breathing at will, but overcontrol injures us. People who need to feel always in control get anxious easily and their breath becomes shallow; if they try to take a deep breath they strain, pushing out their chest and raising their shoulders. They're either unaware or cannot trust that letting go would allow the diaphragm to relax naturally and grant them the ins and outs of a satisfying breath.

Infants don't have this problem. They embody themselves completely, so their bellies go up and down as they breathe, unworried by conflicts and undivided by distinctions. Newborns find everything equally fascinating: their expeditions through the worlds of their bodies have no particular object, and they explore the furthest boundaries of their selves. They grasp their toes and put them in their mouth, they find their nose and ears and suck their thumbs. At first infants find the anus, the penis, the vagina, and urethra not to be particularly special (and much less vital to them than their mouth), but soon they are taught differently. As infants mature into children they are taught distinctions: clean and dirty, forbidden and allowed, male and female.

Many religious and psychological paths make either too much or too little of sex. Sexuality is rather mundane. As physical beings in the order of primates, we are naturally sexual beings. There are many ways of acting or not acting on our sexuality, any of which can embody Rightness—or not.

Sexuality offers an opportunity for wholehearted activity, to fully express yourself through losing yourself in love. Like anything else, though, sex can become contaminated if it serves as a vehicle for self-centered power, greed, and hate. In modern industrial societies people are often divided within themselves, alienated from their work, and separated from their family; because of this sexuality often becomes a substitute for connectedness, a "cure" for the diseases of detachment.

Neither intimacy nor sex is something that can be manufactured, turned on and off artificially, but advertising uses sex to sell the illusion that our sense of inner emptiness can be alleviated through consumerism. The mass media portrays sex as the stimulant that can fulfill you and tries to convince you that physical interpenetration is the same as feeling connected, but this cannot truly satisfy if it does not touch the intimate always-so of interbeing.

So long as we treat sex as a product rather than a natural flow of life's force, we are prone to being alienated from our bodies as well as each other. One cannot reduce sex to a formula (fancy car + ravishing perfume + fashionable vodka = sexual encounter) that can be scheduled on a day planner; one cannot order up an orgasm via an equation (methodical stimulation of the G-spot + application of thrusting technique #4 = pleasure rated as an 8 out of a possible perfect 10). Truly this is absurd.

Sexuality is a form for the intercourse of part and whole. When sex is kindled through intimacy it is like the breath, an inhalation and exhalation of separateness and togetherness, which is most satisfying when it is most Right.

Embodying Rightness takes place at the boundaries of yourself. When you do not need to keep a firm grip on yourself nor clutch onto your lover, when you can abandon yourself to the experience of union without shame or pride, you can more easily attune to each other and find the release of true intimacy. You cannot force this. That which harmonizes intercourse's climax and repose is ungraspable and eternal. Its foundation is deeper than in or out, you or me.

There is no accomplishment or failure in such intimacy, no gain and no lack: only joy.

———

One time when I started meditating at dusk in the Sierras I found the mosquitoes out in force. I tried moving to a place with more of a breeze, but the buggers soon found me. I moved again to a drier patch of ground, but the anopheles accompanied me. I continued to try to meditate but was hyperalert for a buzz by my ear, poised to brush any mosquito away before it could bite. I started feeling annoyed at both the bugs and at my own inability to settle down.

Finally I decided to just do a short meditation and let the mosquitoes bite as they wished. I told myself that most of my body was covered with clothing thick enough the mosquitoes could not bite through; the worst that would happen was that I would itch a lot in a few places. So I ignored the buzzing, relaxed, and let myself sink into stillness without fighting either the mosquitoes or myself.

I enjoyed about forty minutes of meditation focusing on the sound of the nearby stream, its snow-melt rushing to the sea. Afterward I checked myself for bites; to my surprise, I had none. I realized that as I had sunk deeper into meditation, the mosquitoes had buzzed me less and less, letting me meditate undisturbed.

Perhaps meditation changes body heat or pheromones; perhaps, though, the insects did not sting because I'd forgotten myself in the music of the spring.

56

One who knows does not speak;
those that speak do not know.
Seal the openings,
shut the gates,
round the edges,
untangle the knots,
soften the glare,
settle with the dust.
This is called "deep merging,"
"dark consonance,"
"mysterious identity,"
"profound evenness."
You cannot grasp such a One,
cannot push it away,
cannot help it or harm it,
cannot stain or exalt.
Thus *this* is
the incomparably precious
of the world.

WHEN YOU EMERGED from your mother's womb you did not need words to know the world around you; the air that filled your lungs for the first time spoke of liveliness and the arms that held you spoke of love.

When your open eyes focused to take in sights and your ears started to sort out sounds, you began to interpret the sensory data. Interpretation gives meaning to experience but is already one step removed from merging, because it compares one experience with another. Soon language comes along and by separating symbol and significance inherently divides us.

As soon as you say "I" you set yourself apart from the world. Less obviously, as soon as you say "I" you are divided from yourself, becoming both observer and observed. "Who am I?" You can never answer this only through words. Young children faced with this question, though, just laugh and say, "I'm *me*!" When you are being one with yourself, you know who you are, but grasping at the words and ideas you use to describe yourself gets in the way.

Fundamentally, identity means "oneness." When you merge with this ungraspable identity, you reemerge as your true self.

To directly experience your unity, it helps to take a step back and return to yourself. Close your eyes, or keep them open and look within; shut the door and let your tensions unwind of themselves. Turn off the music so you can listen to the swinging gate that is your breath. Soften around the silence, and then let go completely.

When you sit quietly, not doing anything in particular, neither thinking ahead nor thinking back, neither looking out nor in, you can let go of the language of judging. Once you stop comparing yourself to others, you can settle down and relax in a place beyond compare. Your body and mind find each other without a hair's breadth deviation.

You cannot make your one true self better or worse. You cannot run away from your shadow, nor can you chase yourself away; a dog chasing its tail is still a dog. That's why I meditate; I get tired of chasing my tail and need to just sit down and rest.

Stop dividing, stop discriminating, and you find what is incomparably precious. You are precious in a way only you can be. Don't speak of it.

When I was a young man for a while I lived in a Japanese Zen temple. Every morning we'd get up early, vigorously clean the hall, and then sit down for an hour in the dark predawn cold.

During that time I had multiple respiratory infections. Whenever I sat down to meditate my sinuses would fill up with phlegm. I couldn't breathe through my nose and if I opened my mouth the postnasal drip was distracting. Every few minutes I'd take out my handkerchief, blow my nose, then resume meditating until my nose blocked up again.

One day the head monk came to me after meditation and, using his broken English, pointed at my nose, shook his head vigorously, and said, "No blow!" I tried explaining I had a physical problem but he shook his head and repeated, more strongly this time, "No blow!!! No move!!"

So at the next morning's meditation I felt I shouldn't-couldn't-wouldn't blow my nose. Very soon I felt my nose itching . . . getting watery . . . and on the verge of dripping. All my attention focused on my nose and the drip whose fall I fought. I started to sweat, my whole body shook, my hands tensed. Finally, the inevitable happened: MY NOSE DRIPPED and a big drop of mucus fell onto my bare hands.

The initial relief was tremendous, but then something interesting occurred: having let go of what my mind said "shouldn't" happen and let my body be, not only was there no more dripping, but I could breathe freely through my nose. When my body's mind opened up, so did the sinuses of my mind's body.

I realized most of my tension had been due to emotions conditioned by words. How old was I when I first heard "Blow your nose"? How many times had parents or teachers told me how I "should" be bothered by a runny nose? Yet babies and young toddlers, before they learn manners and shame, are able to go around when they have a cold quite unconcerned that their noses are rivers of mucus.

Ever since then when I meditate if I'm ill, usually my symptoms (whether of pain, congestion, nausea, etc.) briefly intensify during the first few minutes of meditation and then abate in some way. Sometimes they come and go and come back, but they no longer interfere so long as I don't get caught by judgments of good/bad, healthy/sick.

Meditation is not a cure—symptoms reappear—but merging body and mind facilitates a nameless state that, nameless, is incomparable. Because it is incomparable, suffering gives way to the simplicity of just being. Snot—like each and all—is incomparably precious, *just this* manifesting as a slimy booger.

57

Govern a state by nothing special;
being crafty is for waging war.
Order all under heaven through noninterference.
How do we know this is so? From this:
The more prohibitions there are, the more rebellious the people.
The sharper the weapons people possess, the more disordered the realm.
The sharper the schemes people employ, the stranger the outcomes.
More laws are proclaimed, then there are more criminals.
So the sage says:
I do not act, and people transform themselves.
I stay in stillness, and people settle themselves.
I have no business, and people prosper themselves.
I let go of desire, and people return to themselves—
simply natural, like the uncarved wood.

WE OFTEN DON'T KNOW how to govern ourselves. This may be why it's so tempting to order others around; it offers a distraction from our own unruly disorders. Perhaps that is why we have so many politicians, middle managers, and administrators. How can you supervise others, though, without first being able to manage your own states?

Of all the modes of governing one's self, perhaps none requires as much sensitivity as the artful discipline of noninterference. We think that to influence the course of events we need to do something special to make an impression on others. We forget that even when we just lie down on the ground we naturally leave an imprint of ourselves. Simply by entering a meeting room, your body changes the air temperature and your mood alters its climate.

We tend to trip over our own feet, stumbling over good intentions and posing problems for ourselves with prohibitions. If you tell yourself not to stare at somebody's birthmark, your eyes will keep coming back to what you are trying to avoid; if you are attracted to someone and want to ask for a date, tell yourself not to stutter and you're liable to get tongue-tied.

Noninterference does not mean passivity: it requires getting out of the way of the Way, not through repression, but through acceptance. Acceptance is not acquiescence or resignation but a matter-of-fact acknowledgment of how things are, independent of our opinions about how they "should" be. The challenge becomes how to face yourself being as you are while facing the world's being as it is, without hope or fear, promises or threats.

Noninterference relies not so much on objective measures as on measured awareness: "What suits this situation?" When you accept something without rushing in to interfere you can see it more clearly and size it up more dispassionately. Sizing something up can include, but does not require, measuring it. Measuring always has its limitations and sharp measures have a way of backfiring. As Chuang Tzu says, "Fashion pecks and bushels for people to measure by and they will steal by peck and bushel." Pass more laws for mandatory sentencing, and you'll have more prisoners, more prisons, and soon an entire industry that relies on punishment to thrive.

Noninterference need not mean inaction, benign neglect, or turning a blind eye to difficulties around you. Intimate awareness discerns how the continuous ebb and flow of change "wants" to go and works with it so that the movement is mutually beneficial. When dealing with a crime wave, encouraging law officers and members of the community to cooperate works better than draconian punishments. If you are raising a teenager, it helps to limit your rules to the most necessary ones and save your energy for the inevitable battles over boundaries as they find themselves. If the forests of California are subject to frequent conflagrations, perhaps you should consider doing less firefighting rather than more: allowing the underbrush to consume itself in small blazes helps prevent calamitous wildfires. Let it be; forests and people naturally return to themselves.

———

I became very fond of a man and woman I had seen for several sessions in couples' therapy. Each of them wanted the relationship to work, and was doing his or her best to be respectful of the other person while remaining honest about his or her own feelings, but somehow each therapy session kept sliding into the same pattern in which misunderstandings piled up and frustrations festered.

One session after trying everything I could think of to help them without success, I asked them if they felt we were getting anywhere. They replied, "No." I asked if they'd permit me to leave the room and wait while I spoke with a consultant to get some suggestions. (This is a fairly common procedure in couples' therapy). They agreed.

I went and found a friend of mine, an expert on couples' and family systems. We spent about ten minutes discussing the situation, and my friend helped me craft a very clever but rather complex intervention that might prove useful to disrupt the couples' usual maladaptive interaction pattern.

I returned to my office, carefully rehearsing the complicated instructions of what I would say to each. I sat down and was about to deliver the intervention when the woman told me she wanted to say something first.

"While you were out of the room, my partner and I discussed our situation and how things are going in the therapy," she said. "We agreed that we both feel you're working much too hard."

"Would it be okay with you to simply sit back for a bit and just let us talk to each other here for a while?"

58

When the government is dull,
its people are wholesome;
when the government is efficient,
its people are deficient.
Good fortune depends on misfortune;
within good fortune misfortune crouches.
Who knows where the pivot point is?
When naturally correct is no longer modal,
straight becomes crooked,
auspicious turns ominous.
People lose their way for a long long time.
Thus the sage is
an edge but does not cut,
a sharp point but does not stab,
a straightforward line but does not overreach,
a light but does not dazzle.

WE DON'T LIKE IT if other people think of us as dull.

Adolescents fear being ordinary more than anything else: better to have an interesting negative identity than to be boring. As adults we revere celebrity until it seems if you want to commune with the stars you need your photo on the front page of *People*, when all you really need do is look up and away from yourself on a dark cloudless evening.

The larger the field of influence, the more the law of unintended consequences applies. Colossal corporations and elephantine governments try hard to manage everyone and everything efficiently. To do this, they establish set procedures and insist people fit into the slots provided. Individual quirks and quibbles get shaved off in order to conform to bureaucracies' categories. This not only frustrates peoples' uniqueness but deprives society of skills that might be a poor fit today but a valuable resource in the future.

Meanwhile, efforts to promote efficiency often backfire; what looks like a straightforward procedure can take crooked turns. Thirty years ago the medical center I worked for needed only one full-time executive administrator to serve two hundred thousand patients; today, with the same number of patients, it has five executive administrators and dozens of managers, one for each clinic. It turns out when an administrator wants to monitor what a doctor does, he creates a form for the doctor to fill out; this form needs more people to review and analyze the information that's been collected; then a manager has to be hired to review the reviewers, and soon managers are needed to manage the managers. Meanwhile, taking the time to fill out forms has made the doctors less productive, so now they are forced to follow procedures standardized for the average patient but are given little time to tweak their treatments to a specific individual's needs or to establish personal relationships with patients. Very few patients fit the average profile exactly, and when they do not fit into their scheduled slots everyone feels uneasy.

We need to return to knowing each other as real people rather than abstract figures in a computer database. You don't have to be brilliant to encourage a little human contact between yourself and whoever you bump into: the client you serve and the person who serves you at the check-out counter at the store, the person who delivers your mail and the cop who catches you for rushing too fast.

Each intersection of your life with others' can become a pivot point that turns your day in either direction, auspicious or oppressive. Which way you go is up to you but as you pivot, there's no need to overreach. Just follow Chuang Tzu's good advice—"Don't stand out and shine, don't go in and hide"—and you will be a light for yourself and for others.

——

When my friend Moshe Talmon first noticed how many of the patients who came in to our psychiatry clinic did not return for any further sessions he assumed this reflected some problem in the treatments we offered. Surprisingly, when he and Michael Hoyt and I researched the matter we discovered most hadn't come back simply because they felt better after even a single session of psychotherapy.

We decided to explore this by videotaping our therapies and doing a formal study of what happened during the first treatment session. We always offered additional sessions, but often a single session turned out to be the only one clients felt they needed.

At first we tried to make clever interventions we thought would maximize the likelihood for clients to get better in their very first visit. We'd consult with each other and, after what felt like a particularly good session with a client we'd sometimes say, "That was terrific! I was really 'on'; I bet it will turn out to have an excellent outcome." We were chastened to discover there was little correlation between our feeling of being dazzling and how well clients actually did. Often sessions where we thought we'd been very sharp turned out to have not-so-great results, while sessions that seemed ordinary and dull resulted in clients experiencing very significant improvement.

I remember one session with an elderly woman who came in complaining of anxiety and depression but who talked so nonstop I literally was unable to get a word in edgewise. At the end of the session she turned to me and said: "So what you're saying, doctor, is that I should take a little more time for myself, be honest with my mother-in-law about our difficulties, and go out and do more pleasurable things with my husband, right?" The only word I uttered during the entire session was my response: "Right." She turned out to have an excellent outcome.

We learned therapy was not about us and what we did: it was about how each *client* made the therapy work. Later research performed in clinics around the world found that even in cases of traumatic misfortune resulting in severe problems, people often are able to turn their lives around in pivotal moments so long as therapists don't get in the way by overreaching.

My Australian friend Colin Riess told me of an experience he had ten years ago when he was first introduced to the possibility of single-session work. He was called in to provide a psychiatric consultation for a seventy-five-year-old man who was a Jewish survivor of concentration camps in Nazi Germany. For the past twenty years the client had been suffering from nightmares four or five times a week. Colin remembers thinking, "well, *this* isn't going to be a single session."

Since Colin didn't really expect the session to lead to anything other than a referral for longer therapy he didn't try to do any sharp interventions and restricted himself to matter-of-fact questions. The session was not terribly dramatic and did not involve reawakening of the terrors of the Holocaust; instead, it focused on the dull details of daily life.

It turned out whenever the client had a nightmare he'd forego taking his usual morning walk with his wife; he said he didn't want to burden her. As the client and his wife talked to each other in the therapy session, though, they decided it would be better, after a nightmare, to be sure to go out on their morning walk and have him tell her a bit about his dreams. By the end of the session they felt hopeful and said they didn't feel a need for further treatment until they'd tried out this new approach. On follow-up, they reported they'd followed through on the plan and felt more close to each other; meanwhile, the frequency of nightmares had decreased to once every few weeks and was no longer interfering with their lives.

I cannot know for certain, but I suspect that if this client had been pushed into longer-term therapy for posttraumatic stress disorder he might have been in for quite an emotional roller coaster. Instead, what had seemed ominous to the client—talking to his wife about his traumas—turned out to be healing. What had seemed to be a tremendously difficult psychotherapeutic problem turned out not to require dazzling treatment techniques; it was open to healing from the light of simple human contact.

59

In governing people and serving heaven
nothing is so good as being sparing.
Sparing, you return before straying;
return before straying, you have Rightness redoubled;
you meet each as it is, and overcome all
in continuous practice not bound by limits.
Knowing no limits means ruling all states;
knowing all states, intimate with Great Mother,
One abides long.
Deep roots, solid trunk:
the Way of clear vision and long-lasting life.

IN OUR SOCIETY of "more is better," being sparing has negative connotations. It has a whiff of ungenerous stinginess, of puritanical strictures against too much pleasure.

Actually, being sparing in our habits spares us distress. If you eat too much, you get a stomachache; if you own too much, you need locks on your doors. Micromanagement produces discontented workers with little initiative; in child rearing, providing your child with every advantage keeps her from learning how to cope with adversity.

Living requires constant adjustments; smaller adjustments are easier and use less energy. You also obtain better results if you don't stray too far. Plumbers know that either tightening or loosening a fitting too much will cause a leak; turning the wrench a full turn in either direction might cause a problem while turning the wrench just an eighth of a turn will accord with the proper attunement.

. Adjustments are not one-time things: we need to be sensitive to what's needed on a continuous basis. Musicians do not tune their instrument once at the beginning of a concert and then forget about it; during the course of a concert the temperature in the hall changes, causing their instruments to go subtly sharp or flat, so musicians are constantly fine-tuning their pitch. Similarly, when raising a child what works at one age doesn't serve for another; just as you've adapted to her developmental needs, she changes and you need to reorient to her new states of being.

The climate of our minds and moods is always changing. It helps to be sensitive to the meteorology of our muscles' abduction and adduction, to the temperature of our feelings' storms and calms that cause highs and lows in our blood pressure. The more we are aware of subtle shifts, the easier it is to recalibrate our activities to match each state.

Continuous practice is a matter of allowing ourselves to be intimately aware of our changing circumstances so that we respond with ease and flexibility. To do this, we need to trust in our ability to adapt. If we don't trust our muscles, we may be afraid to go for a trek; if we don't trust our feelings, we may be afraid to go for a relationship. If we don't trust our minds, we may be afraid to think for ourselves.

Fortunately, we *can* trust in our body and mind to find their place right where we are. If you go to ask a friend for a favor and the set of her eyebrows tells you she's in a bad mood, you'll back off instinctively to wait for a better time and place. If you sprint at the start of a marathon and a twinge in your Achilles tendon warns you to slow down, unless you intentionally overreach (and risk injury) you'll pace yourself as your body needs. We ignore these signals at our peril.

We are deeply rooted in the source of our being as the ebb and flow of our immediate experience, intimately connected to the Great Mother that both engenders and receives us, sends us forth and draws us back. If, uneasy, you wake during the night, reaching for the pillow behind your head—adjusting it a quarter of an inch—allows you to sink back into sleep's restorative embrace. If you are lost in a fog, sit down on a promontory and you won't have to worry about straying from the trail: sooner or later, the sun will burn off the haze, the fog will lift, and you'll be able to see forever.

———

I used to know little of being sparing but was no stranger to strain. Tension and stress seemed to be my normal state; it was hard to undo the knots in my muscles and cramps in my mind.

I learned various coping techniques: progressive muscle relaxation, yoga, body scans, meditation. For the first time in my life, I sometimes tasted what relaxation felt like. Unfortunately, although I usually felt great immediately after practicing any of these, the effect would usually wear off within minutes or hours, and I'd return to feeling tense.

I decided to explore my tension before it had a chance to build up. Each time I became anxious I'd tune in to my body, notice what parts were tight, then ask myself, "If I'd noticed this three or four minutes earlier, which parts would still have been relaxed then, and which would have already been straining?" I gradually traced a chain back from raised shoulders to clenched jaws, from clenched jaws to tight scalp, and so forth.

Eventually the path led to the muscles of my forearm: when these started to tense up, it was a sensitive early warning sign the chain of anxiety was being rattled. At this early stage I found it relatively easy to relax my wrists, plant my feet, take a deep breath, smile inwardly, and interrupt the cascade of tension.

This helped considerably, but still I was often unmindful and over-looked the early warning signals. Then I started practicing qigong and learned the virtues of the qigong hand: fingers spread and gently extended rather than curled; a very slight, natural cup emerging in a relaxed palm; a wide space between thumb and index finger so the hand opens naturally; wrist unbent so hand and arm form a continuous whole.

I spent a year paying attention to what my hands were like throughout the day. I discovered that when I felt irritated or worried my fingers would begin to curl toward a fist; when I was out of sorts my wrist would kink and send my arm (and thoughts) akimbo.

In Zen, we sometimes talk about "opening the hand of thought." Cultivating qigong hand is a concrete way of doing so. Neurologically, a huge proportion of our sensorimotor cortex is devoted to the hand; letting the qigong hand come forth helps ease spread through the whole body-and-mind.

Sparing myself, I am able to spare some attention for others and go easier on us both.

60

Governing a great state
is like cooking a small fish.
Governing the world with the Way,
hungry ghosts lose their power.
Not that they don't have power:
it's just that their power no longer does harm.
Sages harm neither ghosts nor people.
Not harming each other,
Rightness flows between, within both.

OUR FEELINGS are no great states; really they're small fish. They like to convince us they're considerably bigger than they are.

It's difficult to cook a small fish. Leave it on the fire too long and its fillet turns dry; undercook and it is neither sushi nor savory. Similar cautions apply to our feelings. We undercook them when we ignore them; we overcook them when we stoke their fires. If we are anxious, we feel we should be scared; if we are angry, we tell ourselves we deserve respect!

Many of our feeling states are hungry ghosts: residues of undigested yearnings, phantoms of unrequited desires, rejected facets of ourselves. Traumatic experiences can haunt us for generations: your mother may have carried some of her mother's scars and passed them on to you through fits of temper or depression, during which she was unable to respond to your needs. Such past lives may float through your body, mind, and spirit, intermingling with unresolved episodes from your own past.

If you try to reject and suppress these ghosts they are likely to hammer at your door at the most inopportune moment. If you spend too much of your time entertaining the wraiths, you can become a pale imitation of them, cut off from the vitality of current experience. The middle way suggests an alternative: when hungry ghosts come to visit, be a polite and gracious host but do not feed them. The ghosts, being hungry, will depart if they don't find food.

Governing small emotional states can become easier if we treat them as if they were ghosts with their own quirky personality traits. This method is frequently used in narrative psychotherapies. For example, most depressions can be characterized by the following:

- *Depression is a bully.* It is weaker than it appears; its balloon of power can be punctured and defeated by compassion.
- *Depression is a braggart.* It pretends to be self-abasing, but is really all about "me"—convincing the world I'm the very WORST person. Simple modesty and acknowledgment of being only human deflate depression's pride.
- *Depression is short-sighted.* It sees only isolated details. It needs corrective lenses to see the whole picture.
- *Depression is a liar.* It distorts reality to fit its biased picture of the world. It tries to discount discrepant facts but is confounded by matter-of-fact, realistic evidence.
- *Depression is humorless.* It can't stand a joke at its expense.
- *Depression is photophobic.* It shrivels in sunlight and fresh air.

All feelings—pleasant and unpleasant—have a character based in the dings and scrapes, the hopes and fears, of our egos. They pretend to be permanent. In the midst of an emotion, we feel this is how things were, are, and will be, that this is the real state of being and nothing else exists. We can only see as far as our feeling can reach.

In truth, all feelings come and go. Hoping a good feeling will last forever is a setup for disappointment; fearing a bad feeling will last forever is a prescription for despair. Which of your many feeling states is your "true" state of being? The only possible answer is "all and none."

When you are friends with all your feelings—neither ruling nor ruled by them—you are connected to all sentient beings. Knowing your emotions share impermanence with all being, they lose their power to lead you around and harm you. Let them be. Like you, they can find peace in just being themselves; small fish swimming freely in an ocean that easily contains them all.

To quote Chuang Tzu:

> Joy, anger, grief, delight, worry, regret, fickleness, inflexibility, modesty, willfulness, candor, insolence—music from empty holes, mushrooms springing up in dampness, day and night replacing each other before us, and no one knows where they sprout from.
>
> Let it be! Let it be! It is enough that morning and evening we have them, and they are the means by which we live.

Early in our marriage my wife and I had difficulties dealing with the ghosts of angers past. Her parents had been repressed and never argued; my parents had daily screaming matches. My wife had troubles expressing anger; I yelled too much. We got help from a couples' therapist who one day advised my wife: "Next time Bob gets angry and yells, just tell yourself that Bob is having a snit."

I took offense and angrily objected (in other words, I threw a snit). "*Snit?*" I protested. "Snit! That's disrespectful, to belittle my anger like that!"

The therapist smiled slightly. "Well, what would you prefer I call it? A temper tantrum?"

From then on, despite myself, whenever I started to get angry I heard the word "snit" in my mind. It made it hard to use my temper to puff myself up.

At first I was annoyed about not getting annoyed, but soon the silliness of that became apparent. I began to smile whenever I started to get snit-mad. Pretty soon it was difficult to get angry without getting amused, and getting amused was such a soothing anodyne, I stopped getting angry.

I still get mad sometimes, but I usually find it isn't worth the energy. I prefer instead to just enjoy the people I wrestle with—including that most impossible and irritating person: me.

61

A great state is downstream.
Here all rivers meet
the female of the world,
always able to absorb the male through stillness.
Settled, underlying all, she stills.
Great states, by underlying small states, absorb the small states.
Small states, by underlying great states, acquire the great states.
Some, underlying, absorb;
some, underlying, become absorbed.
Great states want to unify and lead,
small states want to join and serve.
For each to get what it wants,
let great states go beneath,
lower and lower.

EMOTIONS MOVE US; great states settle us.

We are so busy we get used to being always on the go, rushing from one thing to the next before finishing the first. Sometimes we feel we're pushing forward, and other times we feel we're being pushed around. Neither is quite correct. It's like one person who sees a flag fluttering and says, "Wind is moving," while another person sees the same thing and says, "Flag is moving." A third person comes and says to both of them, "Mind is moving."

We have many small states of mind, each an evanescent bubble in a larger flow; to the extent we mistake these transient fragments for self-evident truths, we shrink the sea of our self to a small stream. Whether pleasant or unpleasant, all our feelings, thoughts, sensations, inclinations, and flavors of consciousness are ripples on the surface of waters that run deep, tributaries of larger flows. When a friend leaves the area, you can feel happy for them and sad and resentful all at the same time—excited for their prospects, abandoned by their leaving, grateful for what you've shared, and hopeful at meeting again. The more spacious the container for your shared experience, the better your relationship can hold you both.

All the separate currents of ourselves "want" to unite in the great state of our true being. This is not an esoteric mysticism, but how things work: when you run, your arms swing, heels strike, heart pumps, cerebellum balances, and mind monitors your pace, all of them uniting in rhythmic strides. When you are quietly reading you can get so absorbed in a book you tune out everything else. When you are embraced by your love, you join and are joined.

Great states receive and absorb all aspects of an experience but also are affected by what they absorb. The ocean assimilates all that comes to it, but when the streams are full of toxins soon the fish are full of mercury and unsafe to eat. Each baseball team is greater than its players and absorbs them into its group culture, but the team also acquires something from its individual members that alters its collective style. The game of "follow the leader" is a constant give and take that works best when it's hard to tell who is leading whom.

Every moment you stand poised at the meeting of your great and small states. In between one thought and another, after one act and before the next, stop: let your efforts at conscious control relax and allow yourself to be absorbed in the still space where body and mind touch each other.

This stillness is so profound it is endlessly receptive and embraces all that comes to it. However, because we not only yearn for but also are afraid of being absorbed, we often hold back so we won't lose ourselves. Fearing we will dissolve and die if we settle in stillness, we stimulate our separateness; we seek sensational experiences and fire our emotions to reassure us our vital spark is still burning. Doing this, we sometimes burn ourselves out.

It can be difficult to have faith that when we let go of our small states we will not be annihilated but reborn. When we allow ourselves to settle down, though, we find liberation in realizing that letting go does not result in our losing anything. On the contrary: letting go is really letting *be* and offers a serenity so natural it needs nothing special from us, but graces us with stillness in the midst of our moving and being moved.

—

Many of my generation, myself included, grew up in the psychedelic '60s and were initially attracted to meditation through the promise of mind-bending experiences without drugs. Meditation can, in fact, be quite a trip, but you can tell small states are masquerading as great ones when they're accompanied by feelings of grandiosity that resist coming down to the deeper, if more mundane, miracles of everyday life.

My partner Jeanne went to an intensive meditation retreat where they were advised that their lengthy meditations could give rise to unusual mental states, and if they felt lightheaded some sweet food would help bring the meditator back to "ordinary" reality. Jeanne was not too surprised, then, when after several days sitting with four hundred others in the deep stillness of the meditation hall, she heard a voice start chanting slowly but strongly, "*I am Rama! I am Rama!*"

She heard the meditation monitors walk over to the ecstatic meditator and begin to carry him out of the room. As the voice got fainter, she heard the passionate proclamation change: "*RAMA does not WANT a BANANA!*"

Truly great states have room for a bowl of cereal with bananas because the realization of cosmic unity does not obliterate all around it by expanding the individual self. Great states are ordinary and homely, finding each in all and all in each. In Zen we say the absolute and the relative—great states and small—fit together like a box and its lid. We can only experience great states of oneness from the perspective of our fragmented apartness by realizing, in Zen Master Tozan's words, that "I am not IT; IT actually is me." Then you meet yourself everywhere as *just this*—even when IT takes the form of a banana.

The first koan I was given was "How do you manifest your true self in the budding tree?" No special tree is needed, and no special self. In the mountain meadows, an old Hebrew children's song sprang up:

> Who knows One?
> *I* knows *One.*
> One is God, in the heavens and the earth.

62

The Way is the reservoir of rivers, the sanctuary of streams:
a treasure to good people,
a safeguard to those who err.
Beautiful words can be bought and sold,
active honors can be gifted to others.
Why reject even those people regard as no good?
Therefore at the coronation of the emperor
and when the three ministers are appointed,
although there are tributes of jade
followed by teams of four horses,
that's not so good as sitting still and offering the Way.
Thus the ancients honor this Way:
finding meets seeking, straying returning.
One in this Way, world exults in itself.

You CAN FIND sanctuary in your origin, in the all-accepting source of your self.

There are no missteps in this Way. If you slip and fall, the ground catches you; if you get lost in the forest, the sun will still rise in the east and set in the west, providing waypoints for you to recover your bearings.

There is nothing that need be rejected. Each has its place. Flowers are beautiful but lack the green chlorophyll needed to transform the light of the sun into earthy energy; poison ivy may be less welcome in our yard than flowers but still is green as green can be. Leave poison ivy alone and it fulfills its natural functions without harming you. If like a friend of mine you try to uproot all the poison ivy from your front yard, rake it into a big pile, and set it aflame, you run the danger of breathing in its fumes. Then the rash gets in your lungs and like my friend you must go to the hospital lest you die.

We make mistakes. Sometimes we err by trying too hard to spread what we think are gifts: bringing the "good news" of religion to non-European societies decimated local cultures, and planting pretty edible yellow flowers from Europe gave us the dandelions we now treat as weeds. Sometimes we err by trying to control something we see as bad: kudzu was introduced to reduce erosion in earthworks and now is spreading across more than one hundred thousand additional acres a year, activating isoprene, nitric oxide, and nitrogen in a chemical process that produces ground-level ozone.

We make mistakes when we base our judgments solely on the basis of what is personally pragmatic. Everything is vast in its being, but when we focus on a small set of attributes we confuse good and bad with useful and useless. Something may not be useful to you but be useful to another person or another species. If you view things only according to whether they are immediately useful, pretty soon you may need to start worrying about how useful *you* are.

Diversity is vital to a healthy ecology, so nothing is ever useless. "Junk" DNA can hold the key for the emergence of a new trait when changes in the environment put pressure on a species to adapt. When we can value even our mistakes and not reject the seemingly useless results of a mishap, we leave room for new possibilities to emerge: if you forget to clean your lab's petri dishes and on your return don't immediately throw out the strange "no-good" molds that have grown, you may discover penicillin.

Being yourself asks you to have faith that when you stray you can find your way back; to honor your good works but also cherish your bad mistakes; to offer yourself in activity and rest. You will inevitably wander off-track in your doing, but when you stop and sit down, you return to yourself and find your treasure undisturbed.

———

I used to struggle with obsessive perfectionism. If I erred, I'd be harsh with myself, and this often made me irritable with others as well. I feared making mistakes.

When our daughters were eight and four my wife and I took them with us for a few weeks on a European vacation. We rented a car and did a good deal of driving, so we brought a few music tapes to help our children during the long car rides. Both daughters' favorite was the *Sesame Street Sing-A-Long*, which we played again and again, literally hundreds of times until it was more than memorized. One song in particular stuck: Big Bird's "Everyone Makes Mistakes So Why Can't You?"

Shortly after the trip I was walking to my office when I dropped a pencil. I instantly said to myself, "Clumsy!"—but this automatic thought was unexpectedly followed by the song in Big Bird's voice:

> If you spill your milk on the floor
> Don't get upset and shout, just get up and get some more.
> Small people, tall people—matter of fact all people—
> Everyone makes mistakes so why can't you?

I couldn't help but smile. It was hard to be stridently self-critical with Big Bird in my skull.

Listen to Big Bird. Everyone makes mistakes—so why can't you?

63

Do not-doing;
manage affairs with effortless effort.
Know by not-knowing;
savor the flavor of the unadulterated.
Great or small, many or few—
repay wrongs with Rightness.
Deal with the difficult through the easy:
work on the great when it's small,
on the hardest task when it's uncomplicated.
The sage does not try to act great,
thus accomplishes great things.
Those who make promises lightly
seldom keep their words.
Those who think everything is easy
will find many difficulties.
Therefore the sage regards everything as difficult,
and as a result, in the end finds nothing hard.

BEING YOURSELF is not a matter of dos and don'ts.

Doing not-doing does not reside in passivity nor exclude activity: it is the knack of setting your ego aside so there is no separation between the dancer and the dance. Effortless effort is merging with the music of the moment: it is finding and forgetting yourself in flow.

We sometimes put so much effort into our affairs we cannot rest. At night in bed instead of surrendering to sleep we get caught reviewing the events of the past day and worrying about the next. We can become self-conscious and complicate the most basic acts; worrying about how well we'll perform even in bed, we fail to savor the flavor of unadulterated love with our lover. When we turn the episodes of our life into editorials about ourselves, by trying to avoid insignificance and achieve greatness we lose our composure.

Composure is not a feeling but a stance, a way of containing your experience rather than being run by it. It does not separate you from your experience by inducing a phony pretense of calm or numb denial. Composure is not pretending you don't care by reacting to a disappointment with a shrug of your shoulders and a muttered "whatever."

Composure is a form of equanimity. It holds everything we encounter as precious in its own way while handling each in the way it needs. Some experiences are jewels and others are lumps of coal; fundamentally, both are just carbon, shaped into distinctive forms by different circumstances.

We lose our composure when we become attached to our emotions as a matter of rights and wrongs. If we wish to cultivate composure it helps to go beyond tit-for-tat. Piling one wrong on another leads only to more wrongness in widening feedback cycles, which can escalate to violence. If in the face of wrongs we keep looking for our rights, we waste energy seeking revenge; if in the face of wrongs we search for the response that is "just right" we expend the minimum amount of effort necessary.

Our grandiosity is a major impediment to the composure of doing not-doing. Grandiosity makes us exquisitely sensitive to the slights and wrongs we perceive from others; it also causes problems by encouraging us to overreach ourselves. We like to think we are capable of accomplishing a lot, so we make big plans and denigrate the small steps we can accomplish as "too easy." Then we suffer the deflating consequences of not living up to our aspirations. If you make a grand promise and fail to keep it, you will lose faith in yourself; it is much better to just make a small commitment you can be certain to fulfill.

Effortless effort treats everything as equally meriting our full attention but is humble enough to know we cannot force things to our will. Doing not-doing focuses not on achieving great outcomes but on wholehearted engagement and allows itself to appreciate whatever comes forth. This does not take sweat and strain, but it requires careful craft.

It is like working with a diamond. All diamonds have their flaws, but if you examine a diamond carefully and come to know its intricacies intimately, it takes only a small tap at just the right place to split it. This reveals its hidden facets, enhances the gem, and allows it to sparkle.

—

Parenting is naturally easy and impossibly difficult. My next-door neighbor Isabel was driving with her six-year-old son Tom, her ten-year-old daughter Mary, and one of Mary's friends sitting in the back seat of the car. Tom started tormenting his older sister, telling her friend embarrassing things Mary had done. My neighbor told Tom to stop; he'd desist for a little while but in a few minutes would come up with another humiliating story. Isabel again told Tom to stop, but after a brief interlude he came up with another tattletale.

My neighbor began to get angry. She raised her voice and in no uncertain terms told Tom to stop teasing his sister, who was near tears. Again Tom paused but then couldn't resist telling another even more humiliating anecdote. He laughed gleefully as Mary started to cry.

That was enough for his mom. Furious, she pulled the car to the side of the road, strode to the back door where Tom was sitting, and yanked him out onto the sidewalk. Looming over him, she shook her finger in his face and said, "Tom, if you tell one more embarrassing story about your sister, then the next time one of your friends come over I'm going to tell *them* an embarrassing story about *you*."

Six-year-old Tom looked up at his mother with wide, surprised eyes. "But Mommy," he said plaintively, "two wrongs don't make a right!"

64

It's easy to balance while at rest and peaceful;
it's easy to plan while things have not yet arrived;
it's easy to shatter things while they are fragile;
it's easy to disperse things while they are small.
Act before things arise!
Govern before chaos sprouts.
Giant redwoods start from the tiniest shoots;
giant towers start from a basket of dirt;
journeys of a thousand miles begin right at your feet.
But to act is to fail;
to grasp is to lose.
The sage does not act
so avoids ruining things.
The sage doesn't grasp
so cannot be bereft.
Busy people often launch a great project
but just near the point of completion
spoil the work and it fails.
Take care at the end just like at the beginning:
continuous practice never knows failure.
Sages do not desire desire,
do not treasure rare hard-to-get goods.
Sages learn how to unlearn
and return to that which most people pass by.

Sages teach without teaching;
they assist the self-becoming of all being,
just natural, daring to not-act.

CULTIVATING COMPOSURE, you balance each moment by your physical presence. A moment, though, is not midway between was and will be.

Wholehearted activity is not a transition from before to after but complete each moment. If your mind neither anticipates nor hesitates you stand evenly, not leaning forward onto the balls of your feet nor set back on your heels.

When you are sensitive to the needs of the moment you are less prone to procrastination, false starts, and premature terminations. This helps avoid impulsive errors and the need to deal with problems that have mushroomed due to your either ignoring them or impatiently wrapping them up before they're quite finished. If you've ever blurted something out and then regretted it, or pretended a relationship problem didn't exist only to have resentment build to an angry outburst, then you know the virtue of dealing with something before it arises. If you've ever become impatient and, in your hurry to complete a task, made a mistake and had to start all over, you've experienced the importance of finishing one thing before starting another.

Life is easier when you deal with what's right in front of you. This doesn't mean you shouldn't plan: if you have mixed all the ingredients for a soufflé and placed it in the oven, it's a good idea to set a timer so you can check when it's done. It's important, though, to still stay focused in the present. If you fantasize about the finished product while fluffing the egg whites, you run a greater risk of over- or underbeating them and ruining the meringue. If while the soufflé is cooking you're greedy to see the outcome of your efforts before it's ready, opening the oven door too many times makes your soufflé fall flat.

Assisting the becoming of all beings is time-sensitive. Gardeners, artists, parents, and teachers understand that at various times you need to sow seeds or prune off excess; encourage or restrict; initiate or stand back. Your plants will grow, your students learn, and your projects come to fruition if you coordinate your cultivation with their natural proclivities.

Instead of a forced series of stuttering starts and stops, you can find yourself in continuous practice. When instead of acting *on* things you act *with* them, you move in synchrony, and your cooperation makes things easier for both yourself and those you touch.

———

When teaching us qigong Master Hui Liu often found words failed her. She would give us detailed instructions for the intricacies of a movement, but when those didn't suffice she would demonstrate it and conclude by saying "just natural!" We'd be in awe of her flowing grace but think to ourselves, "Sure, for you it's 'just natural,' but for us that movement is really hard." Yet sometimes, if we practiced a movement over and over, at a certain point we'd find the "feel" and whenever that happened we, too, would say—"Oh yes! Just natural!"

When people learn Dayan Qigong, their eagerness to learn all sixty-four movements often leads them to rush through what seem to be the "easy" ones. This is particularly true of the first and last movements. The first movement consists simply of standing, quietly balanced, at rest and peaceful; in the last movement you collect yourself, let the energy settle and distribute itself as needed, and return to standing quietly. I like to tell my students if they can do these two perfectly, they don't need to do the other sixty-two movements of the form. As for me, I've never done them perfectly—but they always help me return to myself.

When qigong students don't take enough time to find stillness at the onset ("Come on, let's get moving!") or rush through the finish ("Done! What's next?"), they don't receive the full benefit of the practice. It's very human to be eager to get going at the beginning of an activity and to be impatient to wrap up at the end, but if we are always looking ahead to what's coming next we miss out on where we are.

Some years ago I was teaching a qigong class, demonstrating a challenging movement. To encourage the students to continue their practice, I said: "This movement is difficult. I have been doing it for fifteen years and am just beginning to understand it. I figure I'll need another fifteen years of practice to master it."

My teacher, Master Liu, happened to be passing through the room and overheard me. She paused, smiled, and said in her accented English: "No no, Bob. Not fifteen years more practice. Whole life, Bob. Whole life."

65

Ancestors, adept at practicing the Way,
tried not to enlighten people
but to maintain them in not-knowing.
People are difficult to rule
when filled with knowledge.
So using knowing to govern the realm
is to steal the nation;
to govern not-knowing
is to be kind to all.
To know these two is to know the universal principle;
to constantly be intimate as principle responds
is Dark Rightness.
Dark Rightness deeply clarifies, reaches everywhere,
returns everything everywhen,
arriving at perfect harmony.

DARKNESS GETS a bad press.

Darkness is a screen onto which we project our dread of whatever we reject; we populate the dark with sinister spirits and hungry ghosts that reflect our ignorance and fear. True Darkness, though, is its own creative being: not an absence of light but an all-accepting, compassionate embrace.

We have feared the dark from the time we huddled in shelters listening to the coughs of hungry predators. We kindle fires to banish the night, but artificial illumination creates its own problems. Burning oil and coal lights up our cities but depletes the dark depths of the earth and pollutes the sky until we can no longer see the stars.

Our desire to dazzle can be problematic. A nuclear weapon's detonation gives off plenty of light but is so bright it will blind you. Knowledge and brilliance sometimes backfire: the Best and the Brightest brought us the Vietnam War, and being (mistakenly) certain of our intelligence regarding weapons of mass destruction led governments into the Iraq war. The sunny cheerfulness of positive psychology sometimes excludes the low bass notes we need to find a more fundamental harmony.

Like moths, we are attracted to the neon signs of nightclubs and the light-emitting diodes of computer monitors and television screens. Our lamps allow us to be productive after the sun has set until we so exhaust ourselves we turn on the TiVo or play a video game to numb our racing minds. When it was still dark at night people gathered around and told tales; perhaps they'd read a book by the light of a single candle or snuff it out to hold one another in the obscurity of love.

Incandescence cannot, by itself, be our essence: it needs the night as a partner. Darkness unites us in our need. During the great Northeastern Blackout of 1965, people helped each other out; New York City experienced its lowest-ever incident of crime. The glistening eddies of a bubbling stream are lovely in their liveliness, but people find it easier to see themselves reflected when the water is dark and unmoving.

Still water forms the mirror that returns us to ourselves. There is wisdom that resides in our dark unknowing, our emotional undertows, our sleep, repose, our unfathomable unenlightened dreams. We need to be intimate with the dark to develop a sense of basic trust.

There are dark moments in our lives when wonder falters in the face of despair, when action is impractical and inaction unthinkable; when need is so great nothing can fulfill it; when pain is so sharp nothing can assuage it; when senseless hate and immensities of suffering cry out for explanation and meaning, but none arises. Here our bright ideas and so-knowledgeable beliefs may crumble. In brightness distinctions become apparent and with them, doubt. At such times we need to keep the faith, a faith tied not to tenets but to something darker, deeper, and more mysterious: the spaces in between.

The dark, in making all things One, unites us with a Rightness larger than our dubious designs. Without knowing who we are or where we are going we learn to trust the Way to wake us in the morning and lull us to sleep in the evening, rehearsing our mortality in the rhythms of our being.

Ultimately light and darkness are a pair, like the foot before and the foot behind in walking. Every moment we appear in the light of the world, we not only throw off an image but cast a shadow. Chuang Tzu reminds us:

> Once there was a man who was afraid of his shadow and who hated his footprints, and so he tried to get way from them by running. But the more he lifted his feet and put them down again, the more footprints he made. And no matter how fast he ran, his shadow never left him, and so, thinking that he was still going too slowly, he ran faster and faster without a stop until his strength gave out and he fell down dead. He didn't understand that by lolling in the shade he could have gotten rid of his shadow and by resting in quietude he could have put an end to his footprints.

——

As a psychotherapist, I initially worked in psychodynamic-uncovering modalities, bringing the unacknowledged to light. It took a while for me to realize that sometimes it was more important to learn what to leave unsaid. I once made a premature interpretation of the unconscious meaning of something a hospitalized client was telling me in a psychotherapy session, and although the client confirmed it was accurate, it frightened him so much he fled the hospital the next day and never returned to treatment.

As a parent, I initially thought it was my job to be realistic and straightforward with my children; I didn't realize how soon the world would bath them in the harsh light of practicalities and how much they needed not accuracy but unconditional admiration. On one occasion one of my daughters, five years old at the time, was singing along with a recording of Ethel Merman (known for her sassy, braying voice) performing a Broadway showtune. My daughter had a sweet but somewhat timid voice, and when she asked me if she sounded like Ethel Merman, I made the mistake of saying "No." Her face fell and her enthusiasm crumpled, and all my attempts at explanation and clarification were ineffective. It might sound like a little thing, but she later told me the hurt of this incident shook her self-confidence and she carried the pain for many years.

Our dreams may not be realistic, but in order to be nourished by their mysterious inspiration sometimes it's best to leave them be.

There was a time when I was scheduled to give a lecture on dreams for a graduate psychology class. I felt conflicted. As a neuropsychologist I was taught dreams are neural discharges which consolidate cognitive processes but have little significance beyond what we assign them when we wake. As a therapist, I was taught dreams are the royal highway to the unconscious. I was unsure what to say.

The night before my lecture, I dreamed that dreams have meaning.

66

Rivers and seas can be kings of the hundred valleys
because they are good at flowing downward;
being lower, they govern all valleys' small streams.
If sages wish to be above the people
they must speak from below them.
Should they be before people
they must be behind them.
Thus when sages are above, their weight does not
    press down on people.
When sages are ahead, they do not hinder or harm
    those behind.
For this reason the world never tires of praising sages
    and pushing them forward.
Because sages are not contentious with anyone
none can contend with them.

WE ALL HAVE our pride. We like to own some special skill or noble quality that enables us to congratulate ourselves and shore up our self-esteem. The problem is that to pride all the world's a stage, and our life becomes a command performance.

We list our exploits in our curriculum vitae and feel the thicker it is, the bigger we are. We sometimes mistake our awards and certificates for merit badges of identity, as if they attest not to what we've done, but to who we are. Being in a prominent position, though, does not make your self better or worse. Two thousand years ago, when selected for the lofty post of premier of all China, Sun-shu Ao said:

> How am I any better than other men? I'm not really certain whether the glory resides in the premiership or in me. If it resides in the premiership, then it means nothing about me. And if it resides in me, then it means nothing about the premiership.

Problems arise when we feel a need to assert our place on the top of the heap as if we were children playing "King of the Mountain," ruling others by pushing everyone else down. We may hope our high position will ensure that people will admire, love, or at least fear us, but we also know it invites others to envy or resent us, and we feel anxious that they'll try to pull us down. Meanwhile there can be a nagging insecurity that whatever you have achieved is not "enough" unless it is an Olympic gold medal or a Nobel Prize. Even then it may not suffice to satisfy our need for admiration and our yearning to feel proud of ourselves.

Pride is not a sin but a self-consciousness. It seriously short-changes you because it sifts your self through filters of important/unimportant, great and worthless. In doing so pride sets you up for its correlates of fear, shame, and humiliation.

There are many ways out from pride. Self-effacement is not one of them; it too easily becomes the unctuousness of a Uriah Heep, a means of covert control. We often couple our coups with a show of modesty: "it was nothing special" we say, hoping others will disagree. Putting yourself down, though, can be a form of pride inverted: if we can't be dominant, we can take refuge in being invested in our submissiveness; if we can't succeed we can take pride in being as bad as we (think) we want to be.

Better to recognize that any identity is a chimera, that because nothing exists except in its interconnectedness, personal pride is an illusion.

All you are rests on all that is; in this web of being, you (like everyone) have your (constantly shifting) place. Stop assigning yourself trophies and booby prizes. Step off the stage and out of the world of comparative value.

The fact is, you are special. Not to acknowledge this is to deny yourself. But as the bumper sticker says, "you are unique—just like everybody else." Each person is special in her own way, in his own particular combination of bigs and smalls and not-at-alls.

Being yourself is naturally vaster than any inflated ego and more durable than pride because it finds itself not in special achievements but in the specks we call our ordinary everyday activities. Folding the laundry, you double back upon yourself. How you speak to the cashier at the checkout counter, how you brush your cat and walk your dog, how you clean your teeth and dust your shelves—each is a complete activity, a field for full actualization.

There's no need to contend with others for primacy of place. It's easier to find intimacy when you let go of pride and stop playing the game of "top this!" When you meet the other person eye-to-eye, you realize yourself with everyone.

———

At one point in my daughter's stormy adolescence, she refused to speak to me for six months. She did not respond with even a word to any overtures I made.

I felt frustrated and upset; as a psychologist, I had an investment in the value of talking as a means to work things out and pride in my ability to empathize and communicate. I tried everything I could think of to break the impasse, but without success. Finally I lost my patience and, utterly helpless, I cried out to her:

"I don't know what to do! I've tried writing letters, and that didn't work. I've tried active listening, and that didn't work. I've tried being silent, I've tried making contracts and agreements, and none of them worked. I've tried everything I can think of and I'm completely out of ideas! I'm stumped! I HAVE NO IDEA HOW TO COMMUNICATE WITH YOU!"

At that, my daughter turned to face me and looked me straight in the eye.

"Good!" she said. "NOW we can make a start!"

So we did.

67

The whole world says my Way is great,

great but useless.

Because it is great,

it has no use.

If it were useful,

it would have long been small.

I have three treasures

to hold, to keep, to care for:

the first is being compassionate,

the second is being sparing,

the third is forsaking being at the forefront in the world.

With compassionate motherly love,

one can be courageous.

With sparseness,

one can be generous.

With daring to not be at the forefront of the world,

one can grow to be a complete vessel, chief of all tools.

If you abandon compassion and yet try to be courageous,

and abandon austerity and yet try to be magnanimous,

and discard unpretentiousness and vie for supremacy,

you will surely die.

One with motherly compassion finds victory in battle

and stands firm in the face of every attack.

What heaven sets up

surround and fortify with compassion's protection.

IF WE NEEDED to be obviously useful in order to live, I'm not certain how many of us would make the cut. Being useful is not necessarily a picnic, either . . .

> Chuang Tzu was walking with a companion when he came upon a huge tree; it was obviously ancient, with a massive trunk and myriads of leafy branches. "What a beautiful tree!" said Chuang Tzu.
>
> "That tree?" replied his companion. "It's worthless! Its wood is too soft to be made into tools; its grain is too knotty to be good to build with. Its fruit is bitter, and when you burn it for fuel or heat, the smell is so bad you'd rather stay cold and eat your food raw. It's good for nothing—totally useless!"
>
> "Ah," said Chuang Tzu. "It sounds like if it had been useful, you would have cut it down a long time ago."

We get seduced by our need to be needed and begin to feel our intrinsic self-worth is tied up with our usefulness. Being productive is an economic mandate but not an existential one. Your worth does not lie in your usefulness, which can only be occasional. If we let our judgments of use and usefulness dictate the meaning of our lives, we can turn against ourselves if we enter an unproductive period or lose a cherished ability even if it's through no fault of our own. This can turn unemployment, old age, and sickness into purgatories of self-loathing.

We have troubles accepting our limits. If the game is on the line and we strike out, we can feel inadequate; if we are invested in social justice and fail to right the wrongs we see, we can feel our efforts are futile; if we want to help someone we care about but feel helpless to do so, we can sink into depression.

The only way I know of dealing with my own and others' smallness, limitations, and useless failures is through compassion. Compassion recognizes our kinship with everyone and everything around us. If we encounter a street musician struggling while their playing is ignored we can be attentive, since we all know what it's like to feel unseen. If we meet a person struggling because they lack marketable skills and can't find work to feed their family, we can be generous: we all know what it's like to feel tired and hungry. If we see even an inanimate object being roughly handled, we can cultivate being mindful in our treatment of things, because we know what it's like to be knocked about.

So much of our suffering—including our attachment to being useful—arises from our wishes to be accepted and acknowledged; we want to be valued, we want others to care about us. Compassion is powerful because when we see compassion in someone else's eyes we know we matter to someone whether we're useful or not, successful or not. We see they care.

Our hearts are limitless but our energies are not. Providers in the helping professions can experience compassion fatigue; if you try to help everyone in everything without recognizing people need to help themselves, your compassion will be more difficult to maintain. If you put yourself at the forefront to lead the charge for every good cause, you'll have to drag anyone behind you who is reluctant. This is grueling.

There is no need to exhaust yourself.

Children, artists, the disabled, and the old remind us we need not be "useful" to put ourselves in play. Like a flower you open to the sun during the day and fold your leaves whenever night falls, harboring the dew and conserving your energy. Have faith in your unfolding. Rest when you need to rest; work when you need to work.

Being compassionate requires nothing extra and takes nothing from you, so you can be generous with others. Being generous depends not on quantity but on sincerity, so there is no excess or lack. When you find your foundation in compassion, you know your life is supported and resonates with everyone else's. You are fortified and surrounded by the good hearts and minds of all around you.

When I returned to work after suffering a stroke I was unable to perform the neuropsychological tests I was supposed to administer to patients. I was subject to fluctuating symptoms such as memory lapses, impaired balance, mental slowness, and apraxias.

I had troubles accepting being useless. On one occasion I became somewhat incoherent while giving a lecture at the clinic; when I sat down at the computer and told my hand to move the mouse, the hand didn't respond. I was scheduled to supervise a trainee in the next hour; being counterdependent I denied my symptoms and planned to keep the appointment. Fortunately a friend convinced me it wouldn't be fair to my supervisee to have to deal with me in my impaired condition.

My colleagues were consistently supportive. They were there for me even when I couldn't perform. I was given a change in duties: instead of neuropsychology, I returned to doing psychotherapy. There I rediscovered that just listening without doing anything special is often better than trying too hard to be useful to a client. Just listening may seem quite "useless," but somehow it seems to be enough; if a person feels heard, his sense of connection gives him courage to continue for another day.

I am deeply grateful for my friends' caring; they helped me learn friendship is not dependent on competency, and compassion is greater than capability.

68

A good captain doesn't show off her might,
a good warrior does not get angry.
One good at conquering enemies
does not instigate combat.
One good at employing people puts himself below them,
  quite humble.
This is called the Rightness of noncontention,
this is called using the strength of others,
this is called uniting with heaven—
ancient perfection.

IF YOU APPROACH your problems as if they were enemies needing to be annihilated, you will be at war with yourself as well as others. We think we need to conquer our problems, conquer ourselves, conquer others. Don't fight so much; life is difficult enough without adding extra strain.

Combat can become addictive. If it is with others you can feel an adrenaline rush as you fight to maintain or regain your place. If it is a struggle with yourself, you may feel a need to test your victories, but reassuring yourself you've conquered a problem by re-exposing yourself to it can be habit-forming. It really is not a good idea for a former alcoholic to enter a bar to demonstrate how well he can resist temptation.

It is counterintuitive, but true, that we have a tendency to become attached to our problems. Our predicaments inflate us: struggling with them helps us feel more alive. So long as we view our trials as tragedies, we can view ourselves as heroes engaged in mythic quests. If we are brave enough to see our hurdles are often merely hiccups, we may feel somehow diminished. When you see your angry tirades as mere snits, it is somewhat embarrassing.

Elevating our misfortunes to the level of calamities feeds their strength. Psychologists call this "catastrophizing." Saying to yourself "this is awful, this is terrible" is very different from saying to yourself "this is unpleasant." Telling yourself "I can't handle this" leaves you in a different place than "at the moment, I don't know what to do."

When I hear a distressed person say "I can't stand this!" I often think "but you *are* standing it, or you wouldn't be able to be here telling me about it." Of course I don't say that, since people who are suffering need empathy, not slaps in the face. Since commiseration magnifies misery I avoid exclamations of "Appalling! Dreadful!" but I do try to provide an empathic reflection that acknowledges the specific pain and immediate hurt without magnifying it into an eternal suffering struggle.

Empathy is not a mere echo; we join with the other person but keep our place, resonating without getting seduced into repeating the exact same tune. If we become submerged and overwhelmed by others' suffering we can't provide the container they need; if we take in their experience from a slight distance, metabolize it and send it back to them in a slightly different form, it can provide the space they need to encounter their experience from a larger perspective.

Empathy is the cousin of compassion; it is a form of noncontention that meets different perspectives by uniting rather than dividing. In doing so it opens channels that allow us, when we face a difficulty, to draw on all our strengths.

It may seem strange to comment on a verse about warfare by discussing empathy. A cardinal rule of combat, though, is to know your enemy. If we can hold off throwing ourselves prematurely into the fray then not always, but most often, we will find that, echoing Pogo, "we have met the enemy, and he is us." At the very least, when we can understand the motives and tactics of whoever and whatever we confront, we gain some better understanding to guide our responses.

The next time you work on a problem, rather than running to wrestle with it, meet it with noncontention. Take some time to stop, stand still, and gather yourself together. With your feet on the ground, draw on the resiliency of the earth; with your head in the air, draw on the clarity of the sky. Relax. Face the problem and let yourself resonate to it and perhaps even empathize with it; allow its reflections within you to ring, flow, fade, and return to silence. Let all the wisdom nested within the experience flow into your hands, heart, and mind; unify them and then, without struggling, in one concerted effort free yourself to be whole and present.

Doing this, it doesn't matter whether the outcome "solves" your problem. Integrated in this way you are beyond winning and losing, because each time you face your problem, you find yourself there.

———

One hot summer day I was working with deep-rooted weeds embedded in rocky hard clay. I tried to dig down but couldn't get very far; I'd grasp the weed's root, pull, and it would break off in my hand. I got very frustrated: what was the use of pulling out weeds when they would only grow back again?

After an hour or so of struggle but little progress, I'd had enough of fighting. I got off my hands and knees, stretched, and relaxed. It was a beautiful day. I looked back at the weeds with a mixture of annoyance, bemusement, and an odd feeling of companionship. I recognized the weeds and I were a match for each other in stubbornness.

When I resumed work I felt more curious and calm. I "met" the next weed, with both my feet planted firmly on the ground, reaching down as far as I could, my hands on its greenery, feeling my way down to its deepest root tip. I closed my eyes and instead of opposing myself to the weed I joined with it, with the soil surrounding it, the earth below and the sky overhead. Something shifted; I felt fully engaged with the weed rather than opposed to it. I pulled *with* the entire weed, root, and stem. It came up effortlessly.

Gone, gone, completely gone . . . until the next spring season perfect with flowers and weeds, sun and sweat.

69

In engaging in warfare there is a saying:
I dare not be the host, better be the guest;
I dare not advance an inch, better to retreat a foot.
This is called marching without advancing;
rolling up one's sleeves without baring one's arms,
wearing no armor, brandishing no weapon, repulsing no enemy.
Of disasters, none is greater than thinking you have no worthy foes;
this brings us close to losing our treasure.
When opponents are evenly matched,
it's the one who feels grief who emerges victorious.

WHAT WARS are you waging? Perhaps you battle with congestion on your commute, fight with obstacles at work, struggle with sticking points in your body or sprains in your mind. Whatever frays you may be facing, they'll get worse if you contend the problem is unworthy and "shouldn't" be there, "shouldn't" bother you, or "should" have a solution.

"Shoulds" are masquerades of desire. We often convince ourselves what we want is how the world ought to be, but our personal views of what's right come not from Rightness but self-righteousness and can easily become a breeding ground of angry resentment. Our "shoulds" can justify turning desires into demands and conflicts into battles.

When we regard an opponent as an enemy we turn our challenger into "the other" and begin to treat him as if he were an object that does not deserve to exist. It is then just a short step to wars that demand unconditional victory, and even "just" wars morph into crusading conquests. When you fight wars of conquest—whether with the problems you have with yourself or with someone else—you not only face possible defeat but also run the risk of losing your heart. You may tell yourself the means justify the ends, steel yourself to collateral damage, and massacre millions in a firebombing that burns innocent and guilty indiscriminately. Mercy can become another casualty of war; unconditional victories may create cruel conditions that plant seeds for future conflicts.

Be careful, though, in condemning combat. Pacifism, too, can turn self-righteous. The antidote to angry "shoulds" is not more moralism but grief.

It is a quirk of human nature that we become attached not just to what we love but also to what we despise. Hate, too, is a form of desire that binds us, one we stick to with a negative rather than a positive glue. This is usually not obvious to us; we rage at a parent who is abusive or abandoning, we revile the pain that nags at us from the body parts that betray us, we curse our disgusting habits and the dark parts of our soul. When they are gone, though, we are surprised to find we miss them. We've gotten used to them as players in the story of ourselves; the very emotional or physical pain we abhored has allowed us to cast ourselves in some role of agonized hero or long-suffering victim. When the dramatic tension is no longer present there is a blank spot in the lines of our script.

The objects of our negative passions are also a part of ourselves, and so the loss of the object invokes not just relief but also a little death. It's difficult to relinquish our wish for a trauma to be transformed; when the parent who disappointed us dies—and all parents inevitably disappoint their children—our wish for the perfect parent dies with them. When the opponent who fails to see the light removes himself from the argument, our wish for a convinced convert leaves with them. In each case a part of us departs as well, and we must grieve the loss of a desired dream.

After a loss love changes form, but the feeling of connection is not annihilated. Even if you lose a limb, you continue to feel its presence: how much more so when you lose someone central to you, a piece of your heart. After a parent, child, or lover dies you find them in the most unexpected places: their favorite dessert, a song they used to hum, the smell on a piece of clothing, or the smile on someone else's face—any of these can recall them to you. At such times, their presence is real despite being incorporeal.

When someone or something we love departs, in grief we are reminded: we are part of everything, everything is part of us, and everything that is part of us is part of us forever. This includes those with whom we've fought, whether these were playful skirmishes or bitter combats. Sometimes the more evenly we were matched, the closer we felt to our dear enemy, whether we acknowledged it or not.

Whatever the outcome of a struggle, we need never lose our human feeling. When we feel hurt by somebody and allow ourselves to experience grief instead of (or along with) rage, we see ourselves in the other and know compassion. The grief that comes from lost love is a reflection of that love's importance to us.

We tend to shy away from grief, which is more painful than fear, more cutting than choler. The paradox of grieving is that it connects us with all living beings in compassion: everyone knows the pain of loss. When we fully come to terms with the loss of a loved person or a dear dream we are on the brink of a great discovery: love is impermanent but eternal. Whoever and whatever we love, we love forever.

———

My sister and I were meditating next to my father when he drew his last breaths and died. A hospice worker started to attend to his body while my sister and I sat next to each other and looked on.

Suddenly my sister sat up as a thought struck her: she turned to me and exclaimed, "It's your birthday!"

It was. As I started to think about what it meant for my father to die on my birthday, I began to anticipate that all my future birthdays would be marked by sadness and I started to feel sorry for myself. My sister turned to the hospice worker and said in a voice of mixed pity and grief, "It's my brother's birthday!"

The hospice worker turned to look at me, caught my eye, and smiled. "How *wonderful!*" she exclaimed.

How wonderful, indeed, to have birth and death so intimately intertwined: what a gift connecting father and son. In that moment, my grief turned to gratitude.

70

My words are easy to understand,
easy to put into practice.
But no one can understand them,
no one can put them into practice.
Words have ancestors;
actions are governed.
Because people don't understand this,
they do not understand me.
Those who understand me are rare.
Those who follow my teaching are preciously few.
Thus sages wear coarse cloth,
keeping jade close within, near the heart.

EXPLANATION IS NOT UNDERSTANDING. Understanding is a felt experience: explanation is too often an excuse.

We like explanations because they are not as risky as direct experience. We can talk about something without feeling too much; by reformulating concrete events into abstract ideas we can avoid putting our body or mind on the line. Medical professionals can elucidate textbook syndromes without understanding what their patients are going through; economists can construct elegant models irrespective of ensuing unemployment; politicians can proclaim ideologies justifying wars more easily when they're not on the ground themselves facing bullets and bombs.

Even when we get involved we don't just sense an experience but also re-present it to ourselves in words and images. In doing so we step outside our experience, substituting observation and formulation for immersion. Then we are literally beside ourselves: separate from the vitality of our flowing lives. We draw lines around our experiencing by forcing it into words, but every word is a boundary that captures some aspects and leaves out others.

It helps to see clearly into the limitations of our perceptions and understanding. These limitations are not restricted to language. Looking at the sky, you do not see the sky—you see a translation of energies transmitted from your retina through your optic nerve to your visual cortex, which converts it to an "understandable" picture. This understanding is incomplete; your nervous system is sensitive to a small set of wavelengths which does not include the infrared or ultraviolet, let alone the vast reaches beyond. The sky is not a colored blue backdrop, but a vast living space.

Similarly, when you look at yourself, you can only see a limited image; when you look at others, your understanding is constrained by the wavelengths of the words and actions you exchange.

How can you understand yourself? Your eye cannot see itself and your mind's self-reference falters in infinite strange loops. We cannot fully understand something as simple as an atom, much less the complexity of our own mental and emotional complexes. Since you cannot fully understand yourself, how can you fully understand another person?

Fortunately, you do not have to understand your life in order to live it, nor do you have to understand your practice in order to deepen it. You do not have to understand another person to love him or her. Although each of us and all around us are mysteries as limitless as the sky and as self-contained as the earth, still we resonate to each other. We pick up on how others feel and sometimes even can anticipate their thoughts. We see someone injure herself, and we wince; even when someone is out of sight we can sometimes feel him smiling and find ourselves smiling in turn.

Empathy and compassion are the foundations of our practice of being ourselves. This practice is simple but not always easy. It urges us to treat everything we meet as precious and allow ourselves to resonate to it, no matter what or when or where it might be. Knowing you can never fully understand, you practice without grasping at familiar certainties.

When you do this, you never become jaded. No matter how many times you have seen someone or something before, in the setting of this particular time and this specific place it is unique. You can refresh yourself by meeting it anew each time, holding it with the curiosity, respect, and care all being calls for. This is putting yourself into practice, together with all beings. It is realizing yourself through the jewel of your heart.

—

Walking with my friend one day he told me he'd recently been depressed. I asked him what was bothering him and he replied with a certain degree of ironic bemusement, "I had my sixty-third birthday a few months ago. I'd always thought that by this age I'd have figured things out. I've realized I've not only not figured things out yet, but it looks like I'm not going to."

I empathized and reflected how the cliché seems true: the older I get the less I know. I admitted to him I had not "figured things out" either, but I felt rather grateful about it: I thought life might become boring if I "figured things out."

I also thought of my friend's good heart, how many people he had helped through his work as a physician and as a teacher, how he had helped raise three wonderful children while still finding time to play the banjo and learn the intricacies of woodworking. He has realized himself in a full life, despite not having "figured things out." It reminds me of a Zen story:

> Once a monk asked Gensha, "I hear you have said 'all the universe is one bright pearl.' How can I gain an understanding of that?"
>
> Gensha replied:
>
> "All the universe is one bright pearl—what need is there to understand it?"

71

Knowing not-knowing: transcendence.
Not-knowing knowing: suffering.
Sick of sickness?
Take care of the one who does not ever get sick.
To say this another way:
to know you don't know is best,
not to know you don't know is a flaw.
The sage's not being flawed
stems from his recognizing a flaw as a flaw.
Flawless!

KNOWING YOU *can't* know encourages the open-mindedness central to scientific inquiry, artistic exploration, and the humility that enables us to feel compassion for others and ourselves. On the other hand, knowing that you *can* know the Way by practicing it—even though you don't fully understand it—gives you confidence to continue on your path.

Knowing and not-knowing encourage each other when they cooperate; if they turn one-sided and go their separate ways both become distorted by pride and prejudice. Knowing that preens itself on certainty becomes ossified into dogmas and ideologies; not-knowing that celebrates ignorance clings to simple slogans and sound bites.

We fool ourselves if we think knowledge is sufficient for curing our ills. Even if we educate ourselves in the skills of our trade, we are not guaranteed success; even if we memorize all the books on how to be a good parent, we cannot ensure our children will be happy. Even if we meditate, there's no guarantee of attaining unsurpassed perfect enlightenment.

The problem is, the more you think you know what's "right," the more you'll see what's "wrong" and get sick of it. If you focus on reforming society, the more certain you are about what is needed, the more glaring the failures of the current situation will be. If you research a medication you are taking, the more you'll learn about (and probably start to experience) its side effects. The more you focus on perfecting yourself, the more your imperfections will become apparent.

You can spend a lot of thought and feeling on what's wrong with you, but there are limits to how helpful this can be, and constant self-improvement can become an obsessive illness. We need to balance our bettering by cultivating a healthy appreciation of inherent flawless being. There is a Zen koan:

> When Dongshan was unwell, a monk asked, "You are ill, teacher, but is there anyone who does not get ill?
>
> Dongshan said, "There is."
>
> The monk said, "Does the one who is not ill look after you?"
>
> Dongshan said, "I have the opportunity to look after him."
>
> The monk said, "How is it when you look after him?"
>
> Dongshan said, "Then I don't see that he has any illness."

When you look after the one who does not get ill you don't have to look far. Healing happens naturally. When you get a cut you need to clean it, put some salve on, and bandage it, but it is not the salve that heals the cut but rather your body's inherent ability to generate new flesh and bone. In the face of fear and failure it is our innate tendency to get up in the morning that keeps us going for another day; we are all endowed with this deep-rooted courage. A crying child eventually stops on his own and resumes play; his ability to play is unlearned and natural, though the more he feels loved, the sooner he will feel able to return to himself.

We want to be healed, but experts on illness cannot satisfy our yearning for health. We require something deeper than a cure; we yearn to know that even as dusty mortals there is something in our being that shines eternally bright no matter how much we obscure it; that even in a world of pain and illness there is a source that cradles and consoles us.

We are all flawed: ephemeral, deluded, incomplete. This is wonderful. Being incomplete enables us to connect with others. Our flaws make it possible to love and be loved; we can resonate to each other's pain and yearning and light up at a glimpse of each other's divine spark.

———

After a hard day at work I felt irritable and tired; I didn't want to attend my qigong teacher training class that night, but I forced myself to go, hoping to just listen to the scheduled lecture. When I arrived it turned out the lecture had been replaced with a practicum during which Master Hui Liu (Shimu) would pick a student to demonstrate and correct his qigong movements while everyone else observed and took notes.

That night she chose me. I wasn't happy about this but got up, performed the movements, and of course got everything wrong. Shimu corrected me again and again, but every time I tried something it was flawed. No matter how much explanation and demonstration I was given, I didn't "get it." This went on for two hours.

Shimu is generous, kind, and gentle, but also insistent. She kept me working on the movements for another hour after the other students had all left. I went on stumbling and bumbling. Finally she smiled and said, "Enough." I thanked her for her teaching but silently thought, "Why did she have to pick me tonight? Yuck! Well, at least it's over."

I left the studio and walked out into the night but had not gone more than fifty yards when I was surprised by a full-body feeling of energy so strong I stopped in my tracks. I could feel warmth and aliveness flowing and circulating through every blood vessel, every neuron, and every muscle, tendon, and bone; each cell in me felt vibrant and awake.

I stood there, marveled, and thought: "*This* is *health!* Up until now I've only known health as a word that meant 'not-sick.' This is different. This is being fully, completely, alive."

Everyone has this health at their source. It is not created by ourselves (though practice helps realize it) nor is it received from a teacher (though teachers can help you get in touch with it). It underlies all and appears unexpectedly even from our awkward missteps.

I don't "understand" it, but having tasted it, even when I'm sick, unhappy, and cannot experience it fully, in the midst of my flaws I gratefully feel my way back toward it by continuing my practice as best I can.

72

When the people fear no power,
disastrous power will soon pay a visit.
Don't restrict where people dwell,
don't oppress how people live.
If you don't weary them,
they will not weary of you.
Thus sages know themselves
but make no show of themselves.
Sages love themselves
but are not full of themselves:
they reject "that" and choose *this*.

WE OVERVALUE WILLPOWER; we think our inner strength should suffice to counter even powerful outside influences. This is a mistake. Psychological research has shown our ego habitually overestimates its strength as part of its illusion of being in control.

Nature is powerful and we are subject to her whims; social systems are powerful and we are subject to their pressures. Habits are powerful and we are subject to their patterns. We swim in seas of conditioned reflexes, workplace politics, family dynamics, guns, and governments.

If you associate with people who are habitually petty or greedy, it will be hard not to absorb some of their impact. If you practice meditation, qigong, or yoga in a garbage dump it won't feel very good. One can be compassionate to people who are harmful, and one can compost garbage, but you don't have to spend your life immersed in either.

Oppression takes many forms: power plays are not restricted to military dictatorships, authoritarian bosses, and thought police. Oppression can be subtle and infiltrate even benign intentions. Sometimes it takes the form of well-meaning advice issued as commands: "Eat your vegetables!" we say to our children. "Get up and exercise!" we say to ourselves. Our teachers may say, "Practice! Practice!"

Commandments can easily become oppressive and turn kindly guidance into coercive control because there is a gap between the intent and the impact of a communication. Every communication has at least three levels to it: the content (what is being expressed), the feeling (the emotion of the person saying it), and the relationship message. This last level is the least obvious and most crucial. "Eat your vegetables!" can be said as a threat, as a suggestion, as a plea, as a joke, and a hundred other variations; whether it constitutes oppression depends on whether it is used to impose the will of one person on another.

Unfortunately whenever we are on the receiving end of coercion we tend to internalize the experience: for example, people who were physically abused as children tend to be terribly severe with themselves and also at risk for abusing their own children. Practitioners of a craft who served harsh apprenticeships tend to impose similar suffering on their own trainees, whether they be sleep-deprived medical residents, athletes taught "no pain, no gain," or meditators forcing themselves to sit still.

When we coerce ourselves we do not love ourselves, and our internalized oppression can come out in subtle ways. We inadvertently impose ourselves on other people: proselytizing a brand of politics, meditation, religion, or exercise; insisting our children excel as a fulfillment of our own projected desires; cutting someone off on the freeway or even staying at a party later than your host would like—all these can be oppressive. We aren't even always aware of how we mistreat ourselves; we can fetter ourselves through obsessive self-criticism that masquerades as self-improvement and chain ourselves to unbridled indulgence that masquerades as well-deserved rewards.

Perhaps the best early warning sign of oppression is a feeling of weariness. You can tell if you are oppressing others if you see they are becoming weary of you; you can tell if you are oppressing yourself if you become weary of yourself. You can tell if you are acting from compulsive willfulness if you become tired quickly and find it hard to press on. You can tell if you are persevering from liberating willingness when, if you start to flag, you find yourself drawing on hidden wells of energy you didn't even know were there.

When we love ourselves but are not full of ourselves we leave space for the flow of energy that comes from our connection with all being. Then we are able to draw on the kind of freedom oppression cannot touch and find compassion even for our purported enemies. People such as Nelson Mandela have shown us it's possible to find this freedom even while imprisoned and persecuted. I don't know if I'd be able to do that, but I have faith that the more I practice knowing my true self, the more I feel comfortable with both myself and others. This seems a good antidote to oppression.

Intimate with yourself, you have no need to act as a dictator to yourself. Intimate with others, you have no need to impose your will on them. True love is true liberation.

—

Sometimes when I get enthusiastic I unintentionally come across as too "know-it-all" and full of myself. I have learned others can find this oppressive.

At work team meetings in our stressful medical center I'd often point out that a problem we faced in our team was part of a larger social or institutional issue. During an off-site retreat, some of my colleagues complained they felt lectured to when I did this. One person said, "While we're all trying to work on the problem of the tree in front of us, it's not very helpful for you to start talking about forestry."

I had an initial impulse to defend myself by explaining how I'd hoped giving a larger perspective would ease some of our frustrations. Then I realized that if my colleagues were finding me wearisome, my good intentions didn't matter much.

So I just said, "You're right. I do tend to jump to the big picture. I'm sorry if this irritates or frustrates you. I'll try to stop, but could you please give me some help? When you notice me doing it, could you let me know right then?"

This turned out well. I'd still sometimes slip into my old habits, but then one of my friends or I myself could say, "Forest!" and we'd laugh.

73

If you're brave in being daring, you'll be killed;
if you're brave in not being daring, you'll live—
one beneficial, one harmful.
Heaven abhors what it abhors—
who knows the reason?
Even a true person is baffled.
The Way of Heaven
doesn't fight or contend, yet easily prevails;
doesn't speak, yet wisely responds;
without being beckoned, comes of its own accord;
is unhurried, at ease, yet patterns a plan.
The net of heaven is vast, all-embracing,
its mesh widely spaced, but nothing slips out.

WE LIKE OUR LIVES to be sensational, so we stimulate our senses with risk. Extreme sports enthusiasts dare extreme injuries, motorcycle racers fly in the face of head trauma. We also like our lives to feel safe: we give up cigarettes to guard our health and install lightning rods to ground our homes. The more we shield ourselves from danger, though, the more we stoke our fear; the more we titillate ourselves with terror, the more we feed our addiction to thrills.

Yet who lives and who dies remains a mystery. Sky divers and dirt bikers usually survive their adventures unharmed, and caution cannot shield you from catastrophe. My nonsmoking mother died of lung cancer while the smokers in her office lived on; my sister's paper boy wore a helmet while bicycling but was struck by lightning and killed during his deliveries.

We may turn to ideology, philosophy, or religion for reassurance, but nothing will save us from the flux: Republican or Democrat, vegetarian or carnivore, faithful believer or atheist skeptic, nature will not discriminate when the earth warms (or cools), when droughts burn barren fields or rains inundate villages with landslides. Our lives' fluid dynamics are capricious, roiling our feelings and tossing our minds and bodies about until they are rounded like river stones.

Understanding will not enable you to control the world and sidestep the flukes of life and death. You may understand the mechanisms of your lungs' alveoli and your cardiac muscles' contractions, but when the telomeres of your cells reach their preappointed lengths this knowledge will not provide you another breath or a single heartbeat more. You may know the endocrinology of sex hormones but be helpless in the face of an overwhelming passion.

Being "good" will not make you invulnerable to disease, assure you of job promotions, or protect your children. Even being yourself will not add or subtract one iota from your life; it will only make your perceptions a bit more keen, soften your heart a little, deepen your dark places until they sound the depths, and brighten your shining to reflect your experience more clearly.

You can't know what life holds for you. You can only face it fully. This takes courage. Courage is not a matter of daring life to do its worst or begging it to bring its best. Courage is being willing to find your place exactly where you are, even when you are baffled by unexpected reprieves and puzzled by surprising setbacks.

That which embraces all is that which prevails. The same source that brings you life and happiness brings you death and despair. It doesn't matter what you call it: God, Buddha, Allah, Tao, the universe. For now, let's call the net of heaven "Nature." You can try to shield yourself from Nature, but any control you exercise is transient; you can worship Nature, but any sacrifices you offer will not ensure rewards. Nature cracks through and wears down all our efforts to shape the world to the direction of our own preferences.

Fighting doesn't help. If instead of battling with yourself you can be courageous and compassionate enough to accept yourself fully, you'll find that, being natural yourself, you are not just kin to Nature but are Nature itself. If instead of fighting with circumstances you have the courage to accept them as they are you'll be better able to respond wisely rather than willfully.

Things have a way of naturally working out, but this happens at Nature's pace and in Nature's Way, not ours, so sometimes we cannot see the pattern. This does not mean no pattern exists. Whether beckoned or not, Nature calls for nothing but comes of itself.

When you find a way to accord with whatever comes, you find Nature is so interconnected, no thing stands alone; there is no thing that is ever lost, no thing that has no place. This includes you.

———

As a young man I relished being daring; I courted risk to counter my phobias of weakness and vulnerability. I bicycled without a helmet, hiked alone in the mountains, climbed up waterfalls with no thought to how I'd descend; I forded streams without proper protection even though I sometimes slipped and was nearly swept away. I enjoyed telling tales of my brushes with disaster but suffered no serious injuries.

I became more cautious once I grew older and had a family. I started wearing a helmet; sought out companions for my hikes and packed a first aid kit, compass, extra clothing and food; I practiced qigong and meditation to stay healthy; when I went trekking in Nepal or India I kept my immunizations up to date and took along a trove of medications in case of illness. None of this prevented me from having a stroke.

After I recovered sufficiently from my stroke, the Himalayas still

beckoned to me. I sought advice from experts in high-altitude medicine about the dangers of returning to the mountains but was baffled
when half the doctors I consulted told me there would be no increase
in danger of another stroke while the other half cautioned me not to
risk it. I finally decided I would go and face whatever Nature had in
store for me. I was willing to turn back in case of warning signals but
also willing to die doing something I loved.

I was fortunate. When I returned to the Himalayas I remained
healthy enough to go wherever my route took me. Sometimes I encountered obstacles—bad weather, recalcitrant bureaucrats unwilling
to issue permits—that required aborting a plan; once I found myself
so fatigued after several weeks of tough trekking, even though it was
at fairly low altitudes, that I felt unable to keep up with my younger
companion and had to drop out early. Other times things have gone
smoothly through icy cirques and rocky glaciers crossing passes 6,000
meters high on the Great Himalaya Trail. Regardless of whether a trek
succeeded in its objective or not, though, on each trip happiness has
visited unexpectedly: in the rose hips gracing a high desert bush, in the
good weather after rain, a basin of unmarked snow, or a simple meal of
dal bhat after a long day.

I don't know if I'll die on a mountain trail, in a hospital bed, at the
wheel of a car, by water or by fire. I am quite certain, though, that if I
try to slip out from or struggle against the net of life-and-death it will
snag me, and so long as I embrace it, it will contain all I bring to it.

74

If people do not fear death,
why threaten to kill them?
If people feared death
and we captured and killed all who acted abnormal,
who would dare to do strange things?
Killing belongs to executioners.
To replace the true executioner
and yourself take on the job of killing
is to replace the master carpenter
in the job of hewing wood.
You are likely to hurt your own hands.

IT IS DIFFICULT to fully enjoy life if you fear death. There are so many ways to die. The Jewish holiday of Yom Kippur has a prayer that lists, in the coming year, "who will live and who will die; who will die by water and who by fire, who by sword, who by beast, who by famine, who by thirst, who by storm, who by plague, who by strangulation . . ."

Since we cannot avoid our mortality, all told it's better to be aware of death than ignore it. If we are not alive to death, we can't fully appreciate the fragility of existence and may not cherish it fully.

Once you accept death's inevitability you can shift your focus from prolonging your life—more is not necessarily better—to doing whatever is necessary to fulfill your being. Sometimes this requires

a willingness to die. If you are committed to a political cause, it may
be more meaningful to die before a firing squad than to betray your
friends and live a little longer. If you are in the midst of a famine, you
may choose to give nourishment to your child even if it risks your own
starvation. These actions are dramatic in their self-sacrifice but there
are many other kinds of death, less fatal but still frightening, you may
need to confront.

Often to go forward we must leave a part of ourselves behind, be
willing to endure a little death that we may live. No comedian can
become a good performer without first experiencing what it's like to die
on stage. Lovers know what it's like to die to each other in a passionate
embrace; those who cannot abandon themselves to this are doomed to
loneliness. In prayer or meditation, in hiking in the meadows or in sipping a cup of tea, if you cannot let go of yourself completely you cannot
fully open to the wonder in which you are immersed.

Confronting your fear of death can be an antidote to anxiety: there
is no need to hold your breath when you can open your heart. When
you are aware of death but do not let it hinder you, you deprive death
of its sting. Take away the gripping dread of the disappearance of your
"I," and you see your way more clearly. Facing death with open eyes
whittles it down to an ordinary event you share with all being, a necessary mystery that is not necessarily miserable.

It's impossible to go through life without killing and being killed.
When a child gives you his still-wet watercolor and you thoughtlessly
say, "Oh my, your clothes are a mess!" you can kill a little piece of his
spontaneous creativity. If you call yourself a "stupid idiot" when you
make an error, you can kill a bit of your ability to experiment freely.
Even those on a strict vegan diet take the life of plants; those plants
in their turn relied on the death of organic life to provide the soil for
their growth.

Whether you are the killer or the one being killed, knowing we all
are prone to little murders can help us be more compassionate for not
just the victims but also the murderers. Most murders are impulsive

acts. Not so the death penalty, which takes years to carry out. Even though the death penalty has been shown to be ineffective as a deterrent to killing, some people feel we should nonetheless retain it in the interest of "justice." However, there is an unavoidable problem in executing murderers: if you make a mistake, it is irrevocable.

Our knowledge is always limited, both of what has happened and what will happen. Retaining the death penalty, it is inevitable we will sometimes execute an innocent person. Death being irreversible, we should respect its awesome nature.

When people defend the death penalty saying an awful deed "deserves" an awful punishment I sometimes think of how, in Tolkien's *The Lord of the Rings*, Frodo says Gollum is an evil creature, a murderer who "deserves" death, and Gandalf replies:

> "Deserves it!" I daresay he does. Many that live deserve death. And some that die deserve life. Can you give it to them? Then do not be too eager to deal out death in judgment, for even the very wise cannot see all ends.

We cannot foresee all the results of our actions. We can know, though, that when we take on the burden of dealing out life and death, the consequences to us will not be trivial. We all do some strange things, and all of us have some Gollum in us. If we start eliminating the obvious Gollums, it is difficult to know where it will stop.

———

After my sister Barbara died at six months old my mother became quite depressed. Sometime between then and my birth three years later, my mother became pregnant. My parents were not able to deal with the possibility of another child at that point and had an abortion. This was at a time when abortions were illegal, shameful, and dangerous.

I don't know many details about the abortion. I know it was hard for them. I also know my parents only wanted two children: if Barbara hadn't died and if my mother hadn't had the abortion, I wouldn't have been born a few years later.

An infant and a fetus perished so that I might live. How can I not treat death with awe?

75

Why are people hungry?
Because rulers levy too much tax on their grain.
Then the people starve.
Why are people hard to govern?
Because governors rule by forceful action.
Then the people are unruly.
Why do people think little of death?
Because they think so much of life.
Then the people don't contemplate death.
One who in living does not pursue any thing
is wiser than one who too avidly grasps at life.

WHAT DO YOU hunger for? If you have unsatisfied cravings, it is hard to govern yourself. Societies stumble when the economic structure is regressive and the power structure discriminatory and oppressive. Individuals falter when they tax themselves too much to obtain what they want or force themselves too hard to suppress their desires.

If we eat when we are hungry and sleep when we are tired, we generally feel satisfied. Our society, though, encourages us to eat when we are not hungry and stay up even when we are exhausted. Our economic order is built on a consumerism that depends on creating needs beyond the necessary, and our political processes are polarized by a small number of people doing very well while a substantial portion of the population is unemployed, underemployed, or a paycheck away from being homeless.

Capitalism creates wealth magnificently but concentrates it dangerously. A business executive, banker, or hedge fund manager who gets paid eleven million dollars a year is earning over five thousand dollars per hour—more than six hundred times the current federal minimum wage of seven dollars and twenty-five cents. It is hard to govern a country when people working at the bottom earn so much less than people doing business at the top.

The mass media fuels conspicuous consumption with images of the lifestyles of the rich and famous; advertisers promote glamour and goods as gateways to satisfaction. "More more more" becomes the mantra, not just of companies seeking to sell goods, but of everything in society: health care offers elective procedures and designer drugs even as millions cannot afford basic services; churches become megacongregations while faith, hope, and charity become commodities. I see even Zen centers straining their resources to provide more classes, more sessions of meditation, more affinity groups to satisfy every perceived need.

Confusing our cravings for needs leaves us with a chronic, nagging sense of deprivation. It's easy to fall into an ongoing state of dissatisfaction and unease, a chronic pain that is difficult to remedy because we no longer know what we truly want. We may feel hunger when we're actually thirsty; we may feel lust when we're actually anxious and just wanting a release of tension; we may feel depressed when we're actually simply tired and depleted.

The United States Declaration of Independence says that everyone is endowed with the inalienable rights of life, liberty, and the pursuit of happiness, but if you're always pursuing happiness, you're like a dog chasing its tail: it will forever slip out of your grasp. Then you have neither true liberty nor true life. If you're always seeking freedom from restraint, you will not appreciate how structured forms can facilitate your practice of the Way. If you're always grasping at life, death becomes a feared enemy rather than the spice that keeps us alert to our fragile existence and the friend who offers peace at the end.

True freedom requires we help each other extricate ourselves from the traps of more and less, of wishing and regretting, of pursuing but never arriving. Both individually and as a collective society we need to stop seeking more, stop grasping to hold on to what we have obtained, and stop pursuing new ways to exploit others in the name of productivity. We need to recognize the gravity of our excess consumption, rebalance the disproportionate allocations of wealth and power, and find the middle Way between suppression and indulgence. We need to cultivate the wisdom of enough.

The root of craving is illusion; the root of satisfaction is the reality that enough is enough.

———

My father lived with us while he was dying of cancer. He loved life; he'd wake up each morning, rub his eyes, look around, then say with a big smile, "Still *here*!" But he was able to contemplate his death peacefully; he said his life had been enough in the people he'd loved and the places he'd seen.

My daughter who was about nine years old was afraid she'd come back from school one day and find Grandpa dead, so I asked my father to have a talk with her. I overheard him reassuring her: he told her he wasn't worried about his death—he had more friends on the other side than on this one—so why should she?

I spoke with her after her chat with my father. "You worried about Grandpa dying?" I asked. She nodded her head "yes." Then I made the mistake of using what I thought was my psychological knowledge. I said, "And maybe you worry about Mommy and Daddy dying?" She replied, "No."

I was surprised and maybe a little hurt. "No?" I asked.

"If you and Mommy don't die," she said, "there won't be room for me and my friends when we grow up."

She's right.

I'm happy to have had my share, and I hope when it's my time to die I will, like my father, be content with enough, not grasp at life, and make way for others to have their turn.

Meanwhile, I've come to realize that my father's "still *here*!" does not just mean "I'm not dead yet." It also reminds us we can be fully alive simply by being deeply present, right here, right now.

76

At birth people are supple and soft:
at death rigid hard, stiff and unyielding.
When plants are alive they are soft, tender, pliant:
when they die they are withered, brittle, and dry.
Thus it is said:
The hard and unyielding are companions of death;
the supple and pliant are companions of life.
So an unyielding army suffers defeat,
a rigid tree breaks.
The hard and mighty grandly dwell below,
the soft and weak humbly find their place above.

OUR RIGIDITIES are the sticking points in our selves. Caught up in the false identities we give ourselves we often don't recognize our recalcitrance; we think "he is stubborn" but "I am strong-willed." We sometimes take pride in our refusal to compromise our beliefs, but this risks turning the warmth of faith into the withering fusillades of fervency.

We can become so unyielding in pursuing our goals that our aspirations become all we are; when we rigidly cling to roles and beliefs we have outgrown we mistake our selves for our memories, and our pasts become penitentiaries.

I've counseled medical residents who had wanted to be doctors since childhood but who, once they started seeing actual patients in busy clinics, discovered they didn't like the work. After so many years of study and so many dollars in student loans they felt being a physician "must" satisfy them, but if they rigidly forced themselves to continue without taking any pleasure in it, both they and their patients suffered. On the other end of the age spectrum I've seen friends in their fifties and sixties who felt tired and burned out from a job they used to enjoy, but kept hanging on "for a few more years" to grasp at financial security. Some of them retired after several miserable years only to see their income evaporate in a bad economy; others died of a sudden illness or came down with dementia before they could enjoy themselves.

Life moves on. Circumstances shift and what we want changes over time. It's not always easy to decide when to carry on and when to let go. Some meditation students persevere at a practice but fail to find the peace or understanding that might come to them if they were willing to stop going down the same path and explore a different one; other meditation students give up just at the cusp of breaking through. On the one hand, discontinuing a practice with "been there, done that" can be due to an unwillingness to commit yourself and a reluctance to put forth wholehearted effort. On the other hand, a sense of "been there, done that" sometimes is a signal that you've become too fixed in your habits and it's time to open yourself to something completely different.

Our futures are unpredictable and our pasts are unrecoverable. If we think we must stick to unalterable goals to secure our future, we may mistake obstinacy for determination. If we think our pasts have molded us into unchanging monoliths we may become rigid and mistake that for consistency. Either way, being unyielding can trap us in brittle images that obscure our living realities.

Fortunately, the dichotomies of stop/start, begin/end, continue/ cease are subsumed in the continuous flowing of our momentary lives. If in the course of your life you find yourself caught between holding on and letting go, you can find freedom in flexibility. Holding on doesn't have to be grasping; it can be a gentle embrace. Letting go isn't giving up, but letting be. In being yourself, it is your willingness to be a stranger to the self you thought you knew that allows you to most fully realize the self you are right now.

———

I come from a family where there was a high degree of both attachment and anger; poor boundaries led to frequent emotional intrusiveness. Because of this, if I'm in a relationship where I feel someone is encroaching on my space, I can become rigid. When I draw a line and say "no further!" this almost always leads the other person to bristle and demand more from me.

While my father was still alive and living some distance away, I would tend to be businesslike on the phone, but he would want to chat. If after ten minutes I said, "Okay, Dad, I'm busy and have to go now," he would reply with "Don't you like talking with me? Can't you make time for your father?" I'd reply of course he was important to me, but continue to insist I needed to go. We'd continue for another ten minutes with me eager to hang up and him eager to hang on.

Finally I decided one day to stretch myself and stay on the phone as long as he liked; however long the call went, I would not be the one to terminate it. So the next time he called, after ten or fifteen minutes when we both ran out of things to say, I didn't start with my "gotta go." A silence ensued. After a pause my father said, "Bob, are you still there?" "Yes, Dad, I'm listening." Without a push-me-pull-you to keep us going, my father didn't have much more to say either; after a few minutes more of chat he was the one who got off the line. Since that time, I felt much more free to stay or go, and our calls became more pleasureable for us both.

I found a similar dynamic came into play in most of my relationships: the more I made myself available, the more the other person felt cared for and the less he or she felt a need to ask for more from me. This was true not just in my personal life but also in psychotherapy. Therapists are usually taught that, when dealing with clients who have poor boundaries, the therapist needs to set very strict limits. I've found that when you set limits, people pound on your door; when you have an open door people feel secure and, knowing you are there for them, feel comfortable being on their own.

Sometimes, though, I still fall into a pattern with people close to me where they feel I am too distant and not sufficiently available, while I feel they're being demanding and invasive. If we each become rigid we run the risk of our warm affection withering and our relationship becoming brittle and dry.

The way through these painful episodes always requires some softening. When we can ease off our inflexibility, embrace our weaknesses, and acknowledge our needs to each other, compassion smoothes our way. Then humbly but with love, we are able to place our relationship over and above the hard sticking points in our separate selves.

77

The way of heaven is like drawing a bow:
what is high is pressed down,
what is low is raised up.
Surplus is reduced,
deficiency is supplemented.
The Way of Heaven
takes away from too much,
adds where there is too little.
The way of humans
takes from those who don't have enough,
gives to those who have excessively much.
Who gives surplus to the world as an offering?
Only those in accord with the Tao.
Thus sages take action but do not hold on to their fruits,
accomplish tasks without being attached to achievement,
do not presume to show off merits or worth.

BEING YOURSELF calls on all of you: it strings together the high and low aspects, drawing them into a continuous arch whose unity spans, reflects, and draws on every part of your body and mind.

Athletes demonstrate this: when a baseball player is up at bat, he plants his feet firmly to provide more upper body strength; when a basketball player makes a jump shot, she knows that the further she extends her legs and feet down, the higher her arms and hands will reach up.

What is true for the body is true for the mind. Enlightenment has its roots in delusion; psychological wholeness requires not just insight from the top down but trust in what comes from the bottom up.

What's true for individual bodies and minds also applies to a body politic and a sane society. We err when we push to maximize the benefit for "me" or "my group" at as high a level as possible while ignoring the people "below" us. Because this is not natural, it is not sustainable: taking from the many who have too little to give to the few who have too much results in economic bubbles that give way to depressions and political upheavals.

In our short-sighted pursuit of personal gain it may not be obvious, but when one person exploits another he depletes not only the other person but also undermines himself. If you elevate yourself by standing on someone else, your increased height will give you further to fall when what is under you moves. You can try to protect yourself in luxurious enclaves, but no amount of personal air conditioning will insulate you from the pollution and global warming that respects no boundaries. Research shows that in societies whose gap between rich and poor is wide, life expectancy and quality of life is lower even for the people on top compared to their peers in more equitable societies.

Greed is not so much sinful as unhealthy. Eat too much and you get sick; carry too much and your back will hurt; grasp at life and your hands will cramp. We all know this at some level, yet it doesn't necessarily prevent us from being self-centered and seeking more money for ourselves, more fame for ourselves, more power for ourselves. Why do we continue to be driven by greed even when we find it fails to satisfy?

Fear motivates us. We fear if we don't have enough money, fame, and power, we'll be vulnerable to the vicissitudes of life—vicissitudes that, in reality, nothing can ensure against. We even fear feeling satisfied, as if it could lead us to let our guard down and erode the walls that guard the stuff we think we're made of.

The truth is that no amount of stuffing yourself will ever fulfill you. There is no security in quantity. No amount of cash will insulate you from a lack of love; no level of fame will pluck you out of the path of a tsunami, and cancer will laugh at your pretensions to personal power. There is no thing whose content, when acquired, can assure contentment.

Contentment depends not on a quantity of things but on the quality of being we discover in generosity of spirit. We find our personal balance by realizing we're all in this together and allowing ourselves to feel satisfied when we have enough. When we have more than enough we can give to others without any thought of return; when we don't have enough we can seek for what we need, without feeling greedy. This is the natural equilibrium that emerges from moment to moment, nonstop flow.

———

During my college years I worked for a while as a janitor. Most of the office workers I served ignored me completely. Once I was changing a light bulb, standing on a person's desk, and she looked right through me; for a moment I felt as if I didn't exist. I vowed then to never repeat that mistake with people "below" me, but I don't always succeed in this.

When I am accosted by a panhandler on the street I sometimes feel uncomfortable. I like to make my charitable contributions once a year, giving a substantial sum to a few causes rather than small dribs and drabs to the many solicitations that come my way. These donations don't make much difference when I am face to face with someone who tells me he or she needs some money for a hot meal; I sometimes have thoughts that get in the way of my genuinely meeting the person. I may think "I gave enough already" or "if I give that person something, what will they use it for?"

Raising the issue of whether the person is "worth" responding to erects barriers between me and the other person. In addition, as soon as

I start judging someone else, my superego kicks into gear and by a sort of Newtonian opposite-and-equal-reaction I start judging myself as well. I can't know what the other person's situation truly is, and to wonder whether he "deserves" a handout misses the point. I'm reminded how in Shaw's *Pygmalion* Alfred Doolittle says that though he is one of the "undeserving poor" his needs are no less than a deserving man's ("people charge me just the same for everything as they charge the deserving"); in fact, his needs are a bit more ("I don't eat less hearty than [a deserving man], and I drink considerably more").

In these encounters, the issue is not one of merits but of meetings, not a question of how much to give but what kind of offering can we make of this moment. I've discovered that when I am able to establish some kind of human contact between myself and the other person, something usually opens up regardless of how much (if any) money changes hands.

For several years my wife and I and our two daughters (then aged eleven and seven) volunteered cooking and serving dinner at a homeless shelter twice a month. The first time we went we were nervous: what would the homeless men be like? We found them to be people like you and I, and—like all of us—more human than otherwise. The men at the shelter were ordinary and friendly; they appreciated the food and our efforts, receiving them without being embarrassed or unctuous. We all enjoyed the conversations we had while we shared food.

There was no special merit nor any shame in breaking bread; my family and I received at least as much from the men at the shelter as we gave to them. We learned that need didn't have to diminish dignity nor did hunger have to trump humanity.

78

In the whole world,
nothing is softer and weaker than water
yet nothing can withstand it.
It wears down the hard and the strong.
Nothing can be used in its stead.
Soft enfolds hard,
weak undermines strong.
Everyone knows this
but no one is able to practice this.
Thus a sage said:
only a person who accepts the country's dirt
can be called its legitimate ruler.
Only a person who accepts the state's misfortunes
can be called its true king.
Upright words sound upside down.

WHEN A RIVER encounters a fallen tree or stubborn boulder the river does not fret about what's in its way but just continues flowing over and under, around and through. In the process, both the course of the river and the shape of rock and branch are transformed.

We humans worry more. We make life more difficult for ourselves. When we encounter a problem we sometimes brood over whether we can withstand it and harden ourselves to overcome the obstacles to our will. In our struggles to be strong we often undermine ourselves. We can get so anxious we forget that by relaxing we become less likely to be injured when we fall; we can become so rigid we forget that our muscles are able to move not just forward and back, but also sideways, up, and down. It's natural to become tense when we hit a snag or confront a challenge but after the initial startle response it helps to soften your stance and relax by taking a few deep breaths.

Most of our difficulties are temporary turbulences, not destructive tornadoes. Of the many issues we struggle with during the course of our lives there are few we'll carry with us in our last thoughts on our deathbeds. Our fears of what might happen often have less to do with reality and more with our images of ourselves: how we think about a problem is a reflection of who we are. The problems we wrestle with need not define us, but the way we face them shapes the paths we choose.

Like water, your true being cannot be broken, but you sometimes may feel torn apart and isolated from the flow of life. Suzuki Roshi likened this sense of fragmentation to what a single drop of water plummeting over Yosemite Falls might feel if it were unaware of its origin in the creek that carried it from the mountain snows and untrusting of the pool below that waits to welcome it back to a larger liquidity.

Water broad at a river's mouth and water narrow at the river's source are each completely water's flowing. In the same way, you are always being yourself. Whether you are four years old or eighty-two, these are merely loci on a greater topography; wherever you happen to be taking place, it is a temporary swirl on a continuous cascade.

This is easy to say but not so easy to feel when you are plummeting out of control. When misfortune comes, we hurt. Disappointed in love, impoverished by macroeconomic forces beyond our control, suffering from painful illness, all the territory around us may look bleak and bad. When we feel inadequate, angry, guilty, or helpless, all the territory inside us may seem blighted and base.

Whether we feel it is the world within that is besmirched and filthy or the world outside that is sludge and mud, we usually want to get rid of muck by denying it or making it disappear. This doesn't work. We have to be willing to get our hands dirty to cultivate ourselves. If we can only tolerate the springs and summers of the world, we'll freeze in winter, let alone miss the pleasures of ice skating and skiing. If we can only tolerate ourselves when being good, we may starve in an anorexic attempt at purity.

To be whole we must accept both our world and ourselves in entirety —spotless and soiled, fortune and misfortune alike. We cannot be the legitimate ruler of ourselves without accepting all we are—which includes the whole world.

———

My friend Robin and I set out early in the trekking season from the Sikkim-Nepalese border in our efforts to map the Great Himalaya Trail, the highest feasible trekking route across the Himalayan range.

For thirty days the monsoon followed us wherever we went. During the first ten days of mud and leeches, I told myself the monsoon would turn soon, the trail would dry, we'd be at higher elevations with beautiful views. The next ten days of mud, rain, snow, and fog brought the disappointment of not getting good views of any of the big peaks around Kanchenjunga. The following ten days brought more mud, sliding slippery scrambles across landslides, and a return of the leeches.

Leeches: wriggling, silent, inexorable seekers that drop off overhanging branches onto your neck and, swaying, inch through all your clothing looking for warm blood. Leech bites are painless but messy (the leech injects an anesthetic and anticoagulant, so sometimes you look down, see clothing stiff with the red of your body, and realize a leech has been feeding unbeknownst to you for some time). Each of us did what we could to protect ourselves from the leeches—sprinkling our boots with salt, covering up gaps in our clothing, rushing through areas of dense foliage to give a leech less time to attach itself—but the annelids with suckers on both ends always found a way to our flesh.

I felt I "shouldn't" dislike leeches and tried to practice radical acceptance. No matter. Leeches continued to give me—and all our crew—
the willies. They didn't hurt, but something about the way they wriggle
and seek, about their blind greediness, perhaps is too reminiscent of
our greedy seeking selves.

I decided to "get into" enjoying mud and get over my aversion to
leeches. By the thirtieth straight day of rain and mud, though, when
we finally reached a shelter where we could take off our filthy clothes,
stiff with mud and blood from leech bites, I stood up and said, "Forget
nondiscriminating mind and equanimity. This SUCKS. And I bet Buddha didn't like leeches either!"

Leeches and mud are not good or bad, right or wrong. But I had to
learn acceptance not only of the bloodsuckers and the muck but also
my unacceptable reactions to them.

Leeches are leeches; mud is mud; and I'm myself, and that includes
the dirty secret that I am still bound by my preferences. I much prefer
wide paths with unobstructed views of mountains. Sometimes, though,
the only path has overhanging branches that drop leeches on the back
of my neck, and the only way possible goes not around but through.

79

Making peace when there's been great resentment,
there's bound to be resentment left over.
How can this be good?
So sages take the poor part of a contract,
make no claim on others.
Those who know Rightness oversee covenants,
those without Rightness implement taxes.
The Way of heaven favors no person in particular
yet Is always with the good person.

WE OFTEN GET RESENTFUL when we don't receive what we feel entitled to.

We make compacts with others and sue them if they don't come through; we make compacts with ourselves and get depressed if we don't make good on our promises. We even make compacts with our gods or the universe and lose faith when fate proves unkind.

There are myriad reasons why compacts break down, ranging from bad luck, incompetence, and unintentional miscommunication to intentional deceit, malfeasance, and exploitation. All contracts, though, are compromises of push-me-pull-yous, so they usually work best when they are most modest. If you are modest in your promises to others you are more likely to find satisfaction in discharging your obligations; if you are modest in your promises to yourself you are more likely to find joy in honoring your intentions. Contracts also often work better if instead of pushing for every advantage you let the other party feel a little bit more satisfied than you are with the arrangement: then they're more likely to follow through on the agreement and if they give back more than you expected, it's a pleasant surprise.

Rationally we understand that contracts and treaties work best when all parties feel they're fair, but we let our anger and greed get in the way. In a divorce, spouses sometimes try to assuage the hurt of rejection by angling for advantage; they wind up embittering not only themselves but also their children. In economic affairs, we know sharing wealth equitably leads to greater social cohesion and fuels economic growth, but this does not stop the rich from getting richer and the poor from getting not only poorer but more numerous. I doubt the framers of the Treaty of Versailles after World War I were unaware that Germans would feel resentment at the reparations exacted, but they still chose payback over peace and sowed the seeds of future wars. Vengeance only spreads the circle of suffering wider. Genuine peace depends on covenants that build trust sanctified by mutual respect. True covenants make life bigger and even holy.

We will not be released from suffering so long as we do things only with an eye to what we'll receive in return; we will not feel truly content so long as we minutely measure whether the scales are even in what we give and get. None of us are totally free of transient twinges of greed, envy, or anger, but once we acknowledge these feelings there's no particular need to hold on to them. Your life is not a matter of exacting what you're owed but of being exactly who you are.

Unlike contracts and covenants, being yourself is completely unconditional: just as the universe is what it is, you are what you are. Realizing this, when you give, you can give unconditionally. When you receive, you can receive unconditionally. Resentment finds no place to arise when you have let go of the concepts of fair/unfair and deal with everything as is best called for. When you stop striving to right your perceived wrongs, you leave room for Rightness to arise wherever you are.

A graduate student of mine, Jose Parapully, did his dissertation on parents who had suffered through the murder of a child. One of the women in his study told him how after the murder of her young daughter the murderer periodically telephoned her at home to taunt her and her husband. The murderer would stay on the line just short of the time it would take to trace his call, and before hanging up he would challenge them to catch him.

The mother went through many stages of grief, fury, and despair. Then one day when the murderer called she unexpectedly felt something melt inside her. She was surprised but found all her expectations and resentments were dissolving and had been replaced by a feeling of compassion. So when he paused a moment in his scornful tirade she broke quietly into the silence and said to him:

"How can I help you?"

There was a shocked pause. Then the murderer broke drown and cried.

He told her of his history of abuse and his tortured sense of guilt and self-hate. She listened and responded empathically. Mercifully, he stayed on the line long enough to be found and apprehended, so others would be protected from him and he would be protected from himself.

When this woman was asked how she had been able to respond as she did, she described it not as a conscious effort but as a sense of clarity that just came to her: the tortured feelings of resentment and anger drained out of her to be replaced by a simple and direct perception of "I just want the violence to stop." This gave her an unexpected, previously inconceivable sense of peace.

She now tells everyone, "It doesn't matter who or where or when or what, it doesn't matter if it's justified or not—I just want the violence to stop."

80

Let the state be small, with a small population.
Though there are efficient machines,
let them be unused.
Let people contemplate death.
Let people not need to move far from home.
Though there are boats and carriages,
let there be no reason to ride them.
Though there be weapons and armor,
let there be no need to display them.
Let people return to keeping their records
   in old-fashioned ways.
Let people be satisfied with their food.
Let them be pleased with their clothing.
Let them be contented in their homes.
Let them be happy with their customs.
Let there be other states so near
people hear their dogs bark and cocks crow
yet people live out their lives with
no comings and goings between them.

THE BIGGEST DELUSION is that self-aggrandizement leads to happiness.
Satisfaction can be found in the smallest act, in the shortest moment.
You do not need to add more to yourself to be more yourself.

Ultimately, being yourself needs nothing special except, perhaps, humility. Humility is not false modesty, nor is it an unctuous self-mortification in which you humble yourself to fight off arrogance. Humility is simply accepting that you do not belong to yourself but to all space and time, all matter and all spirit.

Humility arises naturally when you feel connected to something larger than yourself. You are complete in yourself, but that self is tied ineluctably to everything that lives and dies and sings: the bright light radiating from the fusion of elements in transient stars as well as the dark matter and dark energy of the universe's silent spaces. You sense that your unique body and mind is connected to this vastness and know you belong.

You need go no further than the play of sunlight and shadow to find yourself. Less truly is more. The more complicated your life, the easier it is to get lost; the more cluttered you are by possessions, the more space you'll need. This doesn't mean you must be ascetic and forego pleasure, it just requires you not be averse to pain nor particular about your satisfactions. Being content with enough allows you to appreciate whatever is right before you and feel truly satisfied.

You need no spice other than your mortality to keep your senses sharp and your enjoyment keen. Not making claims on others or on the universe, there is no need to build up your defenses; not constrained by cravings for future fulfillments, there is no gnawing at old bones. You don't have to seek out anything special to have the time of your life: you *are* the time of your life.

Perhaps, nearing the end of this book, you feel disappointed in it, or in me, or even in yourself. There must be something more to life than the simplicity of finding yourself in yourself! Be kind to your disappointment and you will find that when you stop pointing fingers and clenching your fist your hand naturally wants to relax and uncurl. You'll find that, being naturally an openhanded person, your heart and mind naturally follow.

You have your mind and body, the world within and without, being and nothingness, as your teacher. You don't have to understand it, but in reaching for it you express it completely. You are your Way, and it is vast. Always intimate with the Way, you know Rightness beyond speech or thought, action and quiet. Birds sing and you are reborn as song; sleep comes and, dreamless or dreaming, you welcome yourself home.

———

Walking twenty minutes from the busy Tioga road through the high country of Yosemite to the Lyell fork of the Tuolomne, the river meanders lazily through wide meadows. Here the stream is not more than calf deep, shallow enough to wade across; it modestly spills over the smooth granite, forming small pools for children to splash in. It lacks the height of Yosemite falls and cannot rival the glaciated cirques of the Himalaya in drama. It is not so very far from where I live. When I'm done with wandering and die, here is where I want my ashes to be scattered.

81

Truthful speech is not florid,
florid speech is not truthful.
Those who know are not "knee deep in knowledge,"
those who accumulate knowledge do not know.
Goodness is nondiscriminatory,
discriminatory thinking is not goodness.
Sages accumulate nothing.
The more a true person does for others,
the greater the abundance of this True Person.
The Way of heaven:
it benefits but does no harm.
The Way of True Self never contends.
It acts without striving.
Action for others:
forget self and find Self.

AT THE END, there are few words. At the moment of your death, as at the moment of your birth, the truth of your life cannot be expressed in poem or prose: you were, are, and will be one verse in the universe.

You are unique. Every bit of your body is marked by your particular DNA. Your thoughts and feelings are your own; no one can crawl into the spaces in between your ears and pull the strings to control the neurons lodged in your head; nobody can reach beneath your sternum to capture all the impressions beating in your heart.

You share yourself with all existence of all time. The air that fills your lungs has been breathed by trees, Roman slaves, African australopithecines, crocodiles, and algae. The heavy minerals that make up your matter are weighted with the deaths of stars, responsive to the unimaginable pressures that fuse atomic nuclei. You exhale and your carbon dioxide inspires some leaf and modulates the warmth of the atmosphere; you breathe your last and your body feeds the worms to become the soil of others' future food. Speak a word, and its echo may touch someone to an effect generations from now. Take a step, and the ground will never be the same.

You merge with all that is, was, and will be; you emerge again and again in the play of together and apart, same and different, self and other. Always you do this as yourself, dreaming or awake, finding yourself in love or forgetting yourself in the music of activity.

Being yourself this moment, you need not know just what or who you may become. Being yourself this moment, you need not be bound by where you've been.

You are whole: with truly no thing to add and no thing to subtract, there need be no suffering in pain, no striving for achievement, no loss in giving and no gain in receiving. As Chuang Tzu says:

> There is nothing that is not so, nothing that is not acceptable.
>
> For this reason, whether you point to a little stalk or a great pillar, a leper or a beautiful man or woman, things ribald and shady, or things grotesque and strange, the Way makes them all into one. Their dividedness is their completeness; their completeness is their impairment. No thing is either complete or impaired, but all are made into one again . . .
>
> Blowing on the ten thousand things in a different way, so that each can be itself—all take what they need for themselves, but who does the sounding?

Being yourself is Being Itself. Please treasure yourself.

I am grateful to have taken the Buddhist precepts. They inspire us, and serve as guidelines to the Way. It is important, though, that we don't turn precepts and vows into painful strivings for impossible purity. The Tao reminds us to just be natural, to express Rightness by stumbling along in ordinary imperfection, to simply practice not getting in the way of the Way.

At the end of Buddhist lectures and other ceremonies, we recite four vows: "Beings are numberless, I vow to save them; delusions are inexhaustible, I vow to end them; Dharma gates are boundless, I vow to enter them; Buddha's way is unsurpassable, I vow to become it." Lately I have changed the wording of my Buddhist vows, hoping to cultivate an intimate embrace in which Tao and Zen entertain each other with compassion and laughter, truth and beauty. I offer these vows here for you, for me, for everything and everyone:

> Beings are not numbers:
>   the Way is touching all in each.
> Delusions are my self, but creased:
>   the Way is unfolding.
> Rightness is a swinging gate:
>   the Way is unhinging.
> Realization is unfathomable:
>   the Way is flowing, still.

Zen

a separate transmission outside the scriptures
practice-enlightenment mind to mind
the present of presence
faithful beyond belief
freely shimmering
still

Zen (in Chinese, Chan) is a form of Buddhist practice
which emphasizes meditation and the direct experience
of enlightenment in everyday activity. Sudden or gradual,
Zen asks each of us to immediately awaken to our true
nature, genuinely manifesting our original face.

Appendix:

Poems Inspired by
Lao Tzu's Tao Te Ching

Inspired by Verse 16

The sky is an illusion:
The earth its unborn twin.
One moon, two moons?
A never end, a never to begin.

My lover on one side of me
The highway sounds afar:
The daylight hides the brightness
The night reveals the star

So busy, ease-and-worry
Holding on and letting go
All centers touch the Center—
Circumference just So

Stop! Go! Commands are senseless
Still the census of our mind
Uncountable the dusts
Unmeasurable how kind—

that what gives life lives not itself
what kills life does not die.

Still, stillness. Still.

Our laughter, tears are compass points—the pupils of our Eye.

Inspired by Verse 33
For Joel Schone

Not Britain nor the USA could hold
a soul so warm. Binational by law,
by truth a patriot of mountains, Joel
could find his joy no more remote than dawn's

soft touch on village fields, on stony tors,
perhaps a waterfall, whose curtained stream
was portal to such happiness, its core
compassion. For his wages were his dreams

of sharing, knitting friends in scribbled tents
far-flung and local, joined in bad jokes, songs,
life vivid deeply felt and freely lent
to all who journeyed with him. All belonged.

Joel's spirit, vast in Himalayan snow,
enlightened heart: enjoy Ladakh's repose.

Inspired by Verse 37

Some say the good's the enemy of the best;
some say the best is enemy to the good.
But both must serve at striving's strict behest
and miss the finer grain of uncarved wood.

You wish to be ideal, so feel your lack
of wit, your failures loom like moral sins,
while being mortal seems to bring a crack;
the rock of ages split by icy winds

of punishment, reward: delusive puffs
conceal the good is parent to the bad,
desire's twin to suffering. Enough's
enough as earth and sky embrace: comrades

may rest in rightness, free from "don't" and "do,"
becoming's Being: savor being you.

Inspired by Verse 61

A solitary cumulus enfolds to curlicues:
seriously proclaims itself,
punctuates cerulean dreams,
clarifies the sparkling blue.

A single cloud's a comedy
its sensuous swirls too white,
too big to frighten us with fantasies.

Yet if it join its brethren—
massively accumulate,
become still more itself in combination—
might it not convert its maybes into releases:
rainstorms rippling the tempi of our temporary lives?

Sailors ride its streams' returnings,
tides flowing to no profit but a promise:
clear skies tonight.

Inspired by Verse 80

The smallest state is not a thought.
No feeling filters consciousness,
no atom spins in lattices of seeking but
some quirk of ultraviolet
conveys your kind regards amid
the fogs that bridge the valley's crop
to touch the ocean's restlessness
through swells of plankton, krill diatoms
fishermen and astronauts
the chlorophyll of heartbreak—

All serve an unsuspecting wisp
imagination's largest reach
compassion's sweet ungendered child:
what is, is now.

Acceptance of this grace
insists it needs no other place
than mystery. You're here.

Sufficient in your smallest state
ungraspable as joy.
Your body-mind, so actual
is Rightness, Being's mate.

Inspired by Verse 81
A Paraphrase of the Buddhist Heart Sutra,
for Lao Tzu

Compassion practicing deep wisdom
realizes things do not exist, but flow.
Flowing compassion was, is, and will be
completely liberated.
No longer bound, unstuck from misery.
All sincere seekers: seek here-and-now.
Moments are not different from that right before you;
that right before you is not different from moments.
Time and place are ungraspable
but appear only as this time and this place.
Infinite and infinitesimal meet and reflect each other
actualizing the fundamental point.
This is true of all physical phenomena.
This is true of all psychological phenomena.
This is true of each emotion, each sensation,
each perception, each impulse, each thought.
This is true of consciousness,
this is true absent consciousness.
Future's not here; past's in the past;
present moments can never be grasped.
Nothing's pure, nothing's tainted,
no gain and no lack.
Hearing, seeing, smelling, tasting, touching, body, mind:
their appearance is immediate
but they cannot be grasped.
The mind's not a thing; the eye's not a thing;

the nose, mouth, skin, ear exist not as things.
Nose-mouth-eye-ear-skin-mind flow into each other.
Object and subject: two sides of one coin.
This flow never stops, never starts, never ends.
No youth or old age, no birth and no death:
No age but this place.
No place but this now.
Here and now intersect: where they meet, that's the point.
But a point has no width, height, length, color, or sound.
Points have no separation, so there is no illusion.
Without an illusion, no enlightenment breaks.
Not enlightened, not seeking, no nonseparation.
Each is all, all is each.
You're not IT; IT is you.
In a place free from striving, from yearning, from fear:
continuous practice.
Two touching One
One touching Two
without any Three, but relying on wisdom.
Each bell its own sound
Each sound its own bell.
The truth of the truth
proclaims its own mantra
as self speaks its self
a river of music, ceaseless surceasing,
relief, joy, release:
gya te gya te
para gya te
amen, hallelujah
bodhi svaha!

Bibliography

There are many, many translations of the Tao Te Ching. The main ones I used in compiling my version are listed below.

Ames, R., and D. Hall. *Dao De Jing: A Philosophical Translation*. New York: Ballantine Books, 2003.
A somewhat dense and idiosyncratic translation beholden to the philosophical issues the authors want to expound, which occasionally clarify deep implications of a verse.

Chen, E. *The Tao Te Ching: A New Translation with Commentary*. St. Paul, MN: Paragon House, 1989.
Provides extensive commentary, aligning the text with other religious traditions.

Henricks, R. *Lao-Tzu Te-Tao Ching*. New York: Ballantine Books, 1989.
One of the first to use the Ma-wang-tui texts.

———. *Lao Tzu's Tao Te Ching: A Translation of the Startling New Documents Found at Guodian*. New York: Columbia University Press, 2000.
The Guodian texts are fragmentary but may represent one of the oldest versions of the Tao Te Ching. Henricks's scholarly exegesis places them in context and discusses their potential (but somewhat controversial) significance. He compares these materials with the better-known texts, and this sometimes clarifies meanings that were previously obscure.

Hinton, D. *Tao Te Ching*. New York: Counterpoint, 2000.

The most poetic of the translations but also the freest and so the least accurate.

Mair, V. *Tao Te Ching*. New York: Bantam Books, 1998.
A solid translation.

McCarroll, T. *The Tao Te Ching*. Available on http://www.terebess.hu/english/tao/mccarrol.html.
A Christian contemplative's translation.

Red Pine (Bill Porter). *Lao-Tzu's Taoteching*. Port Townsend, WA: Copper Canyon Press, 2009.
The most condensed translation, probably my favorite, but occasionally somewhat idiosyncratic in its choices. Provides helpful brief quotations from classical Chinese commentators.

Star, J. *Tao Te Ching: The Definitive Edition*. New York: Penguin, 2001.
This invaluable resource for those of us who do not read Chinese gives a character-by-character translation, with alternate readings for each character.

Wu, J. *Tao Teh Ching*. Honolulu, University of Hawaii, 1939; New York: St. John's University Press, 1961; Boston: Shambhala, 1989.
One of the first really good translations available, and still one of the best. (Red Pine studied with John Wu.)

Index of First Lines

Index of Subjects

Page numbers in bold type indicate passages in the Tao Te Ching verses. Page numbers followed by "q" indicate quotations from the persons specified.

About the Author

 Robert Meikyo Rosenbaum, Ph.D., has thirty years experience as a neuropsychologist, psychotherapist, and behavioral medicine specialist. He has received lay entrustment in Zen from Sojun Mel Weitsman of Berkeley Zen Center and been authorized as a senior teacher of Dayan ("Wild Goose") Qigong in the lineage of Yang Meijun by Master Hui Liu of the Wen Wu School.

As a psychologist he was chief psychologist at Kaiser Permanente Medical Center; a Fulbright professor at the National Institute of Mental Health and Neurosciences in India; and director of the doctoral training program at the California Institute of Integral Studies. He introduced qigong practice to Kaiser Permanente Medical Center, where he developed numerous neuropsychological services as well as a mindfulness-based chronic pain management program and innovative approaches to brief psychotherapy. He is the author of numerous journal articles, book chapters, and the book *Zen and the Heart of Psychotherapy*. Whenever he can, he spends several months a year hiking in the Sierras and trekking high in the Himalayas of India and Nepal.

About Wisdom Publications

WISDOM PUBLICATIONS is dedicated to offering works relating to and inspired by Buddhist traditions.

To learn more about us or to explore our other books, please visit our website at www.wisdompubs.org.

You can subscribe to our e-newsletter or request our print catalog online, or by writing to:

Wisdom Publications
199 Elm Street
Somerville, Massachusetts 02144 USA

You can also contact us at 617-776-7416, or info@wisdompubs.org.

Wisdom is a nonprofit, charitable 501(c)(3) organization, and donations in support of our mission are tax deductible.

Wisdom Publications is affiliated with the Foundation for the Preservation of the Mahayana Tradition (FPMT).